MILESTONES
IN MODERN
WORLD HISTORY

The British
Industrial
Revolution

MILESTONES
IN MODERN
WORLD HISTORY

MILESTONES
IN MODERN
WORLD HISTORY

600 · · · 1750 ·   · · · 1940 · · · 2000

The British
Industrial
Revolution

ALAN ALLPORT

CHELSEA HOUSE
An Infobase Learning Company

The British Industrial Revolution

Chelsea House
An imprint of Infobase Learning
132 West 31st Street
New York, NY 10001

Library of Congress Cataloging-in-Publication Data

Allport, Alan, 1970–
The British industrial revolution / Alan Allport.
   p.   cm. — (Milestones in modern world history)
Includes bibliographical references and index.
ISBN 978-1-60413-498-8 (hbk.)
1. Industrial revolution—Great Britain—Juvenile literature. 2. Great Britain—Economic conditions—1760–1860—Juvenile literature. 3. Great Britain—History—19th century—Juvenile literature. I. Title. II. Series.

HC255.A73 2011
330.941'08—dc22   2010030579

Chelsea House books are available at special discounts when purchased in bulk quantities for businesses, associations, institutions, or sales promotions. Please call our Special Sales Department in New York at (212) 967-8800 or (800) 322-8755.

You can find Chelsea House on the World Wide Web at http://www.chelseahouse.com.

Text design by Erik Lindstrom
Cover design by Alicia Post
Composition by Keith Trego
Cover printed by Bang Printing, Brainerd, Minn.
Book printed and bound by Bang Printing, Brainerd, Minn.
Date printed: March 2011
Printed in the United States of America

10 9 8 7 6 5 4 3 2 1

This book is printed on acid-free paper.

All links and Web addresses were checked and verified to be correct at the time of publication. Because of the dynamic nature of the Web, some addresses and links may have changed since publication and may no longer be valid.

CONTENTS

The Great Exhibition

It is May 1, 1851, and we are in Hyde Park, central London. Facing us is an astonishing building, almost a million square feet in size, made entirely of glass and cast iron: the so-called Crystal Palace, a giant contraption constructed from scratch in just nine months by 5,000 laborers. Nearly 2,000 feet long and 135 feet high (610 meters long and 41 meters high), the building is so large that full-size elm trees grow comfortably within its three stories. But these are the least of the wonders contained within the Crystal Palace. More than 13,000 exhibits from around the world have been assembled here—foodstuffs, raw materials, precious metals, manufactured goods, tools, and machines—in the largest display of human ingenuity ever known. Today is the opening of the "Great Exhibition of the Works of Industry of All Nations," an event that will go down in history simply as the "Great Exhibition."

The Great Exhibition of the Works of Industry of all Nations was an international exhibition that took place in the Crystal Palace in London, England, in 1851 and displayed examples of all the wealth and technical innovations of the British Empire. Here, the interior of the World Poultry Exhibition at the Crystal Palace exhibition hall is shown.

During the five-and-a-half months in which it will be open, more than 6 million men, women, and children—one in four of the British population—will come to see the Great Exhibition. The admission prices have been deliberately set low to encourage people from even the poorest classes of society to come see the wonders on display at the Crystal Palace. And what wonders! Among the novelties the visitors will see are the Koh-i-noor, the largest diamond ever mined; the world's biggest pipe organ; a stuffed elephant; a giant two-ton (1.8 metric tons) block of steel; a chair made from coal; a carriage propelled by kites rather than horses; an early prototype of the fax machine; a barometer that uses leeches to measure air pressure; and a set of false teeth specially designed to not fall out when the owner yawns. Visitors will work their way through more than 73,000 biscuits (cookies) and 14,000 pounds (6,350 kilograms) of coffee in the various refreshment rooms. Perhaps it is just as well that the Great Exhibition also boasts some of the world's first public flush toilets.

Yet the most impressive exhibits of all are the various examples of machinery—the very latest railroad locomotives, steam engines, textile looms, hydraulic presses, and steamship propellers. Then there are the consumer goods: the clothes, furniture, crockery, kitchenware, tools, timepieces, handicrafts, and other desirable items, which in the mid-nineteenth century are becoming essential to any middle-class household. It is no surprise—and no coincidence—that the most impressive of all of these goods have been made in Britain. For while the exhibition booths in the Crystal Palace are open to all the world's nations—there are representatives from countries across Europe, the United States, even China—the purpose of the exhibition has been to demonstrate Britain's manufacturing skill and might. The Great Exhibition is a celebration of Britain's last 100 years, during which the world has been transformed by a series of technological and economic advances pioneered, on the whole, in the British Isles.

(continues on page 12)

EYEWITNESS ACCOUNTS OF THE 1851 GREAT EXHIBITION

More than 6 million people visited the Great Exhibition during its five-and-a-half-month residency in London's Hyde Park. Among the sightseers was the novelist Charlotte Brontë, author of *Jane Eyre*, who afterward wrote to her father about the wonders of the Crystal Palace:

> Yesterday I went for the second time to the Crystal Palace. We remained in it about three hours, and I must say I was more struck with it on this occasion than at my first visit. It is a wonderful place—vast, strange, new and impossible to describe. Its grandeur does not consist in one thing, but in the unique assemblage of all things. Whatever human industry has created you find there, from the great compartments filled with railway engines and boilers, with mill machinery in full work, with splendid carriages of all kinds, with harness of every description, to the glass-covered and velvet-spread stands loaded with the most gorgeous work of the goldsmith and silversmith, and the carefully guarded caskets full of real diamonds and pearls worth hundreds of thousands of pounds.
>
> It may be called a bazaar or a fair, but it is such a bazaar or fair as Eastern genii might have created. It seems as if only magic could have gathered this mass of wealth from all the ends of the earth—as if none but supernatural hands could have arranged it . . . , with such a blaze and contrast of colors and marvelous power of effect. The multitude filling the great aisles seems ruled and subdued by some invisible influence.*

Like Brontë, many observers were astonished by the sheer range of human goods that had been collected under one roof, evidence of the amazing manufacturing output of the Industrial Revolution. The magazine *Art Journal* described some of these wonders of the exhibition in its catalog:

On entering the building for the first time, the eye is completely dazzled by the rich variety of hues which burst upon it on every side. . . . Forming the centre of the entire building rises the gigantic fountain, the culminating point of view from every quarter of the building; whilst at the northern end the eye is relieved by the verdure of tropical plants and the lofty and overshadowing branches of forest trees. . . . The objects which first attract the eye are the sculptures, which are ranged on every side; some of them of colossal size and of unrivalled beauty . . .

[The exhibition includes] brass and iron-work of all kinds, locks, grates . . . agricultural machines and implements . . . cotton fabric and carriage courts, leather, furs, and hair, minerals and machinery, cotton and woollen power-looms in motion . . . flax, silk, and lace, rope-making lathes, tools and minerals, marine engines, hydraulic presses, steam machinery . . . silks and shawls, lace and embroideries, jewellery and clocks and watches . . . military arms and models, chemicals, naval architecture, philosophical instruments, civil engineering, musical instruments, anatomical models, glass chandeliers, china, cutlery, and animal and vegetable manufactures, china and pottery . . . perfumery, toys, fishing materials, wax flowers, stained glass.

* Quote taken from "Eyewitness: The Great Exhibition, 1851," MyTimemachine.co.uk. http://www.mytimemachine.co.uk/greatexhibition.htm.
** Quote taken from "The Great Exhibition of 1851." http://myweb.tiscali.co.uk/speel/otherart/grtexhib.htm.

(continued from page 9)

"Nobody who has paid any attention to the features of our present era will doubt for a moment that we are living at a period of most wonderful transition," boasted Queen Victoria's husband, Prince Albert, who was one of the chief organizers of the Great Exhibition, at a fund-raising banquet in London two years earlier:

> The distances which separated the different nations and parts of the globe are gradually vanishing before the achievements of modern invention, and we can traverse them with incredible ease; the languages of all nations are known and their acquirements placed within the reach of everybody; thought is communicated with the rapidity and even by the power of lightning.[1]

The exhibition's visitors, no matter where they come from, are living on a planet that has been transformed in the space of just three or four generations by British ideas.

"THE WORKSHOP OF THE WORLD"

Nobody alive in 1851 doubts that Great Britain is, as future Prime Minister Benjamin Disraeli will call it, the "workshop of the world."[2] Nor does anyone seriously question the idea that, in another of Disraeli's memorable phrases, the British have enjoyed "a convulsion of prosperity"[3] during the previous hundred years. The economic statistics tell the story clearly enough. At the time of the Great Exhibition, Britain is producing more than 2 million tons (1.8 million metric tons) of pig iron a year, more than every other country in the world put together. Its textile factories have 21,000,000 cotton spindles, five times as many as France, its closest competitor. Almost 6,000 miles (9,656 kilometers) of railroad track have been laid across the United Kingdom, compared with half that in Germany. Britannia's trade and finance dominate the globe.

Moreover, the British have used their economic muscle to seize large portions of the world's surface. In 1851, the Union Jack flies from the Pacific coast of Canada to South Africa's Table Mountain, from Hong Kong Harbor to Sydney, Australia. The Royal Navy's hundreds of warships patrol every sea and ocean. A few years ago a single steam-powered British gunboat shattered China's entire fleet of war-junks in a single afternoon, bringing an ancient empire to its knees; soon, when the Royal Navy builds its first ironclad battleship, its power will be even more uncontestable. The world order under informal British leadership—the "Pax Britannica," as it has become known— seems secure and permanent.

But what is perhaps even more astonishing than Britain's global leadership in 1851 is how rapidly it has been acquired. A mere 100 years earlier, it was France, not Britain, that seemed to be the dominant power in the world. Britain in the mid-eighteenth century was certainly a nation to be reckoned with, but it had nothing like the financial supremacy that it enjoys in Queen Victoria's reign. A country that a century before still had an economy dominated by farming and agriculture, much as it had been for 2,000 years, has become the world's first industrial giant in just a few generations. What has taken place in Britain is far more than just a growth spurt. It is the dawning of a whole new way of organizing labor and production, a whole new way of thinking about how a society ought to be organized and how wealth can be procured. The results have been, quite literally, revolutionary.

And the results will not be confined to Britain. Already the ideas and innovations of the Industrial Revolution have crossed the English Channel and the Atlantic Ocean. In France and Germany, entrepreneurs are building factories and foundries. In the United States, textile mills and ironworks are being linked to a rapidly expanding railroad network that will soon dwarf anything found in Europe. Even in distant Russia and exotic Japan, ambitious businessmen are planning to import

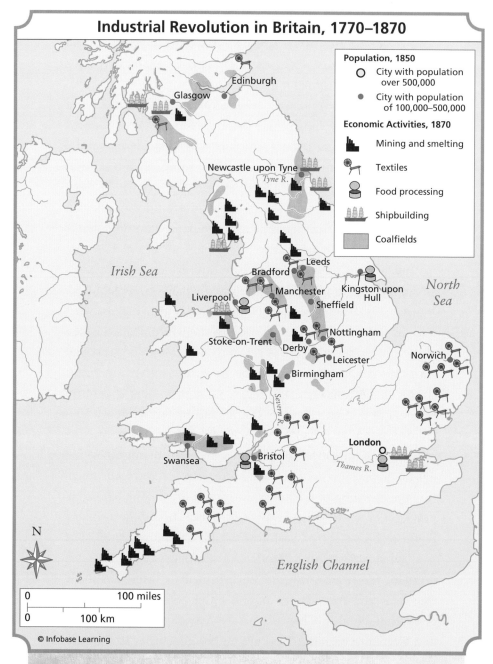

Industrial Revolution in Britain, 1770–1870

Population, 1850

○ City with population over 500,000

● City with population of 100,000–500,000

Economic Activities, 1870

Mining and smelting

Textiles

Food processing

Shipbuilding

Coalfields

Edinburgh

Glasgow

Newcastle upon Tyne

Tyne R.

Irish Sea

Leeds

Bradford

Manchester

Kingston upon Hull

Liverpool

Sheffield

North Sea

Nottingham

Stoke-on-Trent

Derby

Leicester

Norwich

Birmingham

Severn R.

Swansea

London

Bristol

Thames R.

N

English Channel

0   100 miles

0   100 km

© Infobase Learning

Beginning in the eighteenth century, the Industrial Revolution transformed the economy and society of Great Britain. The Industrial Revolution would not have been possible without fuel in the form of coal, of which there was ample supply in Great Britain. By the mid-nineteenth century, half of the world's coal was being produced in Great Britain.

the British template for industrial manufacturing. By the end of the nineteenth century, Britain will find its place as the workshop of the world already challenged by a host of upstart rivals who have copied and improved upon ideas that originated in England, Scotland, Wales, and Ireland. The Industrial Revolution will have become not merely a one-off event restricted to a single country, but the model for the commercial future of the world.

The legacy of the Industrial Revolution that took place in Great Britain between approximately 1750 and 1850 has turned out to be profoundly double-edged. It brought immense wealth to mankind and allowed the production of goods at a rate that was unimaginable as little as 250 years earlier. It altered transportation and communications beyond recognition; a world that relied upon horse-drawn wagons and the written letter was suddenly and irreversibly changed by the invention of the steam train and the telegraph. But its benefits were not equally distributed. For millions of Britons, the immediate effects of the Industrial Revolution were catastrophic: Packed into squalid, teeming cities, men, women, and children spent their short and dismal lives working backbreaking shifts in unhealthy sweatshop factories. So the story of Britain's economic transformation in the eighteenth and nineteenth centuries is also the story of the fight for political and social rights in the face of bewildering and often frightening change, a fight that continues to this day in many parts of the world.

Additionally, while industrialization brought wealth, it also brought environmental destruction. By the 1850s, the River Thames in London had grown horribly polluted from the ceaseless dumping of raw human sewage and industrial waste matter into its waters; the smell grew so bad one particularly hot summer that Parliament and the law courts had to abandon their work, because no one could stand the stench. The famous London fogs of the 1800s, which we romantically associate today with the crime sleuth Sherlock Holmes, were not a natural phenomenon at all, but a kind of yellowish smog built

(continues on page 18)

ALBERT, PRINCE CONSORT (1819–1861)

Prince Albert of Saxe-Coburg and Gotha, the husband of Britain's Queen Victoria, was the dynamic visionary who thought up and organized the 1851 Great Exhibition. An enthusiast for all things creative and technological, Albert devoted his life to the encouragement of reforms and advances in the arts and sciences. In many respects this energetic prophet of progress was the ideal role model for the nineteenth century "Industrial Man"—passionately convinced that knowledge and reason would create a new golden age for humanity.

Albert was born into a family of distinguished but minor European aristocrats. His father, Ernest, was the Duke of Saxe-Coburg and Gotha, a small central German territory less than 2,000 square miles (5,200 square kilometers) in size. The family derived its importance less from its land holdings than from its successful marriages with other European royal dynasties. Albert's uncle was Leopold, King of Belgium, and it was he who first suggested that the teenager might make a suitable bridegroom for his niece Queen Victoria, who had ascended to the British throne in 1837. This politically loaded decision was the subject of intense negotiations between diplomats of the various countries, but Albert and Victoria themselves had no doubts: The two fell quickly and deeply in love. They married in February 1840, with Albert being granted the title of "His Royal Highness the Prince Consort."

Many of Victoria's subjects thought this petty aristocrat from a penniless German duchy was a poor match for their new queen. But a few months after their wedding, Albert was praised for his cool heroism when a would-be assassin shot at him and Victoria while they were out for a carriage ride. Moreover, the prince consort had a sophisticated grasp of public relations. As their family expanded—he and Victoria would eventually have nine children—he carefully cultivated an image of the royal family as the model of domestic respectability.

Albert, intelligent and hardworking, associated himself with progressive ideas. As chancellor of the University of Cambridge, he introduced a modern curriculum, encouraging among other things the study of science. An enthusiast for cutting-edge, even controversial ideas, he championed the work of naturalist Charles Darwin when his theory of evolution by natural selection was still condemned by many churchmen; Albert sought (unsuccessfully) to have Darwin granted a knighthood. The prince consort was also interested in advanced farming techniques and devoted much time to making the family estates efficient and profitable. He steadily took over so much of the day-to-day business of court from his wife that one royal counselor eventually admitted: "He is king to all intents and purposes."*

Albert's participation in and patronage of the 1851 Great Exhibition was the crowning moment of his career. But there was tragedy to come. In the winter of 1861, he caught typhoid fever and died suddenly at Windsor Castle. His grief-stricken wife withdrew from public life for much of the remaining 40 years of her reign. The prince consort's life was eventually commemorated in the massive Albert Memorial erected in Kensington Gardens in London. Fittingly, the memorial is covered with scenes depicting science, technology, trade, and manufacturing—the pursuits that Albert, a champion of the Industrial Revolution, was so keen to encourage.

---

* "Prince Albert," PBS: Empires: Queen Victoria: The Changing Empire. http://www.pbs.org/empires/victoria/empire/albert.html.

(continued from page 15)
up from trapped coal fire smoke; these so-called pea-soupers caused respiratory disorders and killed thousands of people each year. In time, technology and new regulations restored London's water and air to good health. But the environmental havoc caused by rapid industrialization continues across the developing world in the twenty-first century.

Britain Before the Industrial Revolution

Perhaps the best way to see how rapidly Britain changed from the mid-1700s to the mid-1800s is to imagine what an ancient time traveler would have thought of the country before and after the Industrial Revolution.

Suppose a man who lived in Roman Britain (Britain controlled by the Roman Empire) in about A.D. 50, shortly after the death of Christ, was able to travel forward in time to about 1750, shortly before the American Revolution was to break out across the Atlantic. What would he have seen?

More people, for one thing. The British population had roughly doubled in the intervening period from about 3 million to 6 million. London, which had been a tiny Roman colony in the first century, was now a city of about 750,000 people—a very imposing sight, though still quite a bit smaller in size than ancient Rome. Some new technologies would have been

VIEW'S of LONDON. Nº 1.

Entrance of PICCADILLY or HYDE PARK CORNER TURNPIKE, with a View of Sᵗ GEORGES HOSPITAL.

Published ... 1797, by ... Ackermann ... Strand.

In this color engraving of a London streetscape, circa 1797, the capital's muddy unpaved roads are clearly displayed. Prior to the Industrial Revolution, many roads had not undergone serious repair since Roman times.

mysterious and frightening to our ancient visitor. Gunpowder, for instance, would have startled him, though the invention of guns had not changed warfare as much as you might think. Eighteenth-century muskets were only really effective up to 50 yards (46 meters) and took a long time to reload, which means that a Roman soldier armed with a sword and javelin would have had a decent chance of charging a British Redcoat. Our visitor would probably have been more impressed with changes in ship design across the centuries. Great oaken vessels capable of sailing around the globe had replaced the small oar-driven galleys of the ancient Mediterranean. By the mid-1700s such vessels were bringing to Britain rich cargoes of spices and silks from Asia and tobacco from the Americas, continents that would have been unknown to our ancient Roman.

Still, what would probably strike the time traveler as most surprising is how the world had not changed all that much during the 1,700 years that he had jumped across. In many respects, life in mid-eighteenth-century Britain was very similar to what had existed at the time of the Roman emperors. The great majority of the population still lived in the countryside and spent their lives farming the land. Agriculture was the backbone of the national economy, with manufacturing very localized and small-scale. With the exception of London, most towns remained quite small. Most ordinary people lived, worked, and died without traveling more than a few miles from their birthplace. Nature still governed the rhythms and patterns of day-to-day existence. People woke at dawn and worked till dusk, with the day shorter in winter and longer in summer. Movement on land still took place either on foot or by horse; the most urgent message could travel no faster than the quickest rider. Indeed, travel was often *slower* in the mid-eighteenth century than it had been in Roman times, because the roads were so much worse.

Now, let us send our Roman time traveler forward just a little bit further in time—to 1850, rather than 1750. Although only 100 more years would have passed, our Roman would be utterly bewildered by the world around him. Mid-nineteenth-century Britain would seem thoroughly strange to him. The population would be more than three times as large as it had been in 1750. London would dwarf classical Rome. And great cities would have appeared where only small towns and villages had existed 100 years earlier. Bradford in Yorkshire, in which fewer than 4,000 people lived in 1750, now had 182,000 inhabitants. A whole urban civilization had sprouted up, seemingly out of nowhere, in northern and midland England. And in those new industrial

(continues on page 24)

ROAD TRAVEL IN EIGHTEENTH-CENTURY ENGLAND

Before the Industrial Revolution, English people rarely traveled large distances by land, for the simple reason that it was so difficult. No extensive road building had taken place in England since the Romans had departed 1,500 years earlier; the roads that did exist were usually muddy, potholed cart tracks, dangerous and exhausting to traverse. What should have been routine journeys from town to town were more like dangerous expeditions into the unknown. In 1751, for instance, a Dr. Burton of Cambridge wrote in his journal:

Sussex is not easy to ride or drive through. . . . No one would imagine them [the roads] to be intended for the people and the public, but rather the by-ways of individuals, or more truly the tracks of cattle-drivers; every where the usual foot marks of oxen appeared; and we, too, who were on horseback, going on zig-zag almost like oxen at plough, advanced as if we were turning back, while we followed out all the twists of the roads. Not even now, tho' in summer time, is the wintry state of the roads got rid of, for the wet retained even till now in this mud is sometimes splashed upwards all of a sudden, to the annoyance of travelers. Our horses could not keep on their legs, on account of these slippery and rough parts of the roads, but, sliding and tumbling on their way, and almost on their haunches, with all their haste got on but slowly. . . . Come now, my friends! I will set before you a sort of problem in Aristotle's fashion. Why is it that the oxen, the swine, the women, and all other annuals are so long-legged in Sussex? May it not be from the difficulty of pulling the feet out of so much mud by the strength of the ankle, that the muscles get stretched, as it were, and the bones lengthened?*

The celebrated wit Horace Walpole gave an amusing account of a journey he took the following year:

We lay at Tunbridge town. The inn was full of farmers and tobacco; and the next morning, when we were bound for Penshurst, the only man in the town who had two horses would not let us have them, because the roads, as he said, were so bad. We were forced to send to the Wells for others, which did not arrive till half the day was spent. We went to Lamberhurst to dine; near which, that is, at the distance of three miles [4.8 km], up and down impracticable hills, in a most retired vale, we found the ruins of Bayham Abbey. Here our woes increased: the roads grew bad beyond all badness; the night dark beyond all darkness; our guide frightened beyond all frightfulness. However, without being all killed, we got up, or down—I forget which, it was so dark—a famous precipice called Silver Hill, and about ten at night arrived at a wretched village, called Rotherbridge. We had still six miles [9.6 km, to go], but determined to stop. Alas! There was only one bed to be had, all the rest were inhabited by smugglers. We did not at all take to this society, so, armed with links and lanterns, set out again upon this impracticable journey. At two o'clock in the morning we got hither to a still worse inn, and that crammed with customs officers, one of whom had just shot a smuggler. . . .**

* E.M. Bell-Irving, *Mayfield: The Story of an Old Wealden Village*. London: William Clowes, 1903, p. 11.
** Ibid., p. 12.

(continued from page 21)

cities, great smokestack factories, powered by steam engines, would be churning out textiles, ironware, and tools. Men and women whose great-grandparents had worked on the land would now be machine operators swept into the cities by the lure of manufacturing wages. Those cities would not be linked by muddy cart tracks and stagecoaches but by iron railroads. Messages that would have taken days to send in 1750 could be communicated in seconds by the electrical telegraph. Life was conducted not by the cyclical rhythms of nature but by the time-table and the clock—precise, mechanical, and unyielding.

In short, in the space of only three or four generations, Britain had progressed from an ancient way of life to a modern one.

TRADITION, PRIVILEGE, PREJUDICE

Let us take a step back again then and look at Britain on the eve of the Industrial Revolution. Tradition still lay at the heart of so many of Britain's institutions and practices in the mid-1700s. The country was organized in a patchwork quilt of shire counties that had barely been altered since the Middle Ages. High sheriffs and justices of the peace exercised law and order, just as they had for hundreds of years. The king and his court continued to glory in all their ancient pomp and circumstance, adorned with titles and trappings that would have been familiar to medieval monarchs. The two houses of Parliament, the House of Commons and the House of Lords, had seemingly changed little in centuries; many peers of the realm could trace their noble ancestry back 1,000 years, while the constituencies represented by members of Parliament (MPs) in the Commons had not been altered for generations, even though their relationship to reality was often very weak—one MP was supposedly elected by the people of Dunwich, a village that had almost entirely disappeared underwater.

In the mid-eighteenth century, Britain was a profoundly unequal society, with wealth and privileges usually passed down through birth and inheritance. A political economist, Joseph Massie, calculated that the top 18,000 aristocratic families, representing only about one percent of the population, received in income about one-seventh of all the capital in England and Wales. Most of this wealth was tied up in land. Agricultural rents were the key to respectable prosperity. A gentleman was not a professional or an entrepreneur and certainly did not involve himself in anything as unseemly as trade; he made his living as a peaceful country landowner, harvesting his crops and gently squeezing the peasantry of all the money he could get.

And although it had relatively progressive laws compared with many other states in Europe at the time, Britain was still dominated by members of the Protestant Church of England, or Anglican faith. To take part in public life in eighteenth-century Britain, one had to be a practicing member of the national church. Catholics and "non-conformists"—members of non-Anglican denominations like the Presbyterians and the Methodists—could not study at the University of Oxford or the University of Cambridge, sit in the House of Commons, or serve as officers in the army or navy. They were excluded from all government service. Old suspicions of Catholics as disloyal and "un-British" still lingered and occasionally flared up into violence; in 1780, a 60,000-strong crowd chanting anti-Catholic slogans rampaged through London, looting shops and beating up Irish immigrants. Many educated members of society still clung to credulous folk beliefs; John Wesley, the founder of Methodism, was firmly convinced of the existence of witches.

A NEW WORLD OF SCIENCE AND REASON

During the second half of the seventeenth century and the first half of the eighteenth, the scientific revolution swept across the universities and academies of Europe, challenging ancient assumptions about the form and function of the universe and

(continues on page 28)

SIR ISAAC NEWTON (1643–1727)

By formulating the basic laws of mechanics and motion that govern the visible universe, Sir Isaac Newton made possible the intellectual environment in which the Industrial Revolution could take place a century later. Yet Newton was a paradoxical figure—a scientist, a religious mystic, and an alchemist—who wrote much more about prophecy and magic than he did about science.

Newton was born in rural Lincolnshire in the English Midlands in 1643. His father, a prosperous farmer, had died three months before his birth. After Newton's mother remarried, the infant Isaac was dispatched to live with his grandmother. He went to school in the market town of Grantham. Newton's family intended him to become a farmer like his father, but the young man made it clear that he sought a life of study. In 1661, he was admitted to Trinity College, Cambridge. The turning point in his career came in 1665 when the university had to close because of the threat of plague. Newton returned home to Lincolnshire to carry on his research in private. During the next two years, he developed the ideas that would change scientific inquiry forever.

Along with his contemporary, the German philosopher Gottfried Leibniz, Newton is recognized as one of the inventors of the modern branch of mathematics called calculus—the study of rates of change that provides the mathematical tools that are fundamental to understanding the behavior of quantities and objects. Calculus provides the theoretical foundation for all scientific and engineering work today.

Newton took an interest in optics, or the study of light. He proved that the "white" light that we see all around us is not really white at all, but is made up of a spectrum of

In this illustration, Sir Isaac Newton analyzes the colors in a ray of light. Considered by many scholars to be among the most influential men in human history, Newton was a physicist, mathematician, astronomer, natural philosopher, alchemist, and theologian.

colors that can be observed when a glass prism splits a beam of light. He was able to demonstrate that rainbows,

(continues)

(continued)

which were objects of mystery, were simply a natural example of this splitting, or "diffraction."

If these had been Newton's only discoveries, then they would have made him one of the most important figures in the scientific revolution. But it was his work on gravity and motion that really changed human understanding of the natural world and made him one of the most important men in history. Contrary to the charming myth about an apple landing on his head one day, Newton did not "discover" gravity. He did, however, show that all physical objects in the universe obey the same basic gravitational laws. By using a set of elegantly simple formulas, Newton proved that one could predict the behavior of any moving object, from a marble to a planet. By showing that inertia and momentum act in the same way on Earth as they do in space, Newton created the science of classical mechanics that underlies our whole conceptualization of the physical world.

For his work, Newton was elected president of the Royal Society in 1703 and knighted two years later. But Newton's later life was not a happy one. Obsessed with calculating the end of the world with evidence from the Bible, he suffered a nervous breakdown. His eccentric behavior in his final years may have been caused by his occult experiments with toxic chemicals like mercury. Of his great contribution to science, Newton said simply: "If I have seen further it is by standing on the shoulders of Giants."*

---

* Stephen Hawking, *On the Shoulders of Giants: The Great Works of Physics and Astronomy*. Philadelphia: Running Press, 2002, p. 725.

(continued from page 25)

humanity's place in it. This new mind-set certainly did not permeate every level of society, but it did establish a new way of thinking, especially in Britain, which would be a necessary starting point for the Industrial Revolution later on.

Until the mid-1600s, scholars continued to rely on biblical and classical authority—that is to say the beliefs of the Christian church and the views of ancient Greek philosophers such as Aristotle—for their understanding of the natural world. In that era, scholars tended to follow the laws of logic first defined by Aristotle, who perfected observation and classification based on analysis; it would not be until the scientific revolution that the scientific method, based on observation and experimentation, was employed.

Before the scientific revolution, most natural processes were explained as the work of God. Any theories or evidence that contradicted established beliefs—for example, suggestions that Earth might revolve around the Sun rather than the other way around—were regarded as false and often blasphemous. As late as 1600, the Italian philosopher Giordano Bruno was burned at the stake for holding this heretical viewpoint.

By the seventeenth century, more and more scholars insisted on using reason and experimentation to understand natural processes, rather than simply church dogma or traditional beliefs. Building on the earlier hypothesis of Copernicus, German astronomer Johannes Kepler proposed that the planets revolved in ellipses around the Sun and that their movements could be predicted through mathematics. Italian astronomer Galileo Galilei also strongly believed in a heliocentric, or Sun-centered, solar system, which ran contrary to the scriptural interpretations the Roman Catholic Church was making at the time. (Galileo, in fact, held a position similar to that of fifth-century philosopher and theologian St. Augustine of Hippo, who believed that not every passage in the Bible could be taken literally, especially if the scripture is a poem or song and not a book of laws or history.) Although the Catholic Church did eventually censure Galileo for his beliefs, he nevertheless proposed theories of motion that challenged traditional claims about the movement of objects in space.

Britain played a particularly important role in the scientific revolution, partly through the work of individual scientists such as Sir Isaac Newton, Robert Hooke, and the chemist Sir Robert Boyle, and partly through new institutions of research. The Royal Society, founded in 1660 by King Charles II, encouraged the discussion and publication of new scientific work. King Charles later also established a Royal Observatory at Greenwich, which was eventually chosen as the site of the prime meridian dividing the Western Hemisphere from the Eastern.

The scientific revolution was not directly concerned with the economy or manufacturing. The steam engine and the other technological marvels of the Industrial Revolution were still a long way in the future. But it was a vital first step, because it provided the theoretical background that the engineers of the late 1700s would need and established the principle that the world could be understood rationally—that the old ways of doing things were not necessarily the most sensible.

The Capitalist and Consumer Revolutions

On the morning of September 8, 1720, an excited crowd gathered outside the Merchant Tailors' Hall in the Cheapside District of London. Inside the hall, which was packed to bursting by a clamoring throng, the directors of the South Sea Company opened an extraordinary meeting that they hoped would calm the fears of their panicking investors. It was no accident that the meeting had aroused such passions: For thousands of shareholders, the fate of the South Sea Company was going to mean the difference between prosperity and disgrace in debtors' prison. London, which for months had been in the grip of an investing frenzy, was about to discover an ugly truth of finance: the bigger a speculative bubble grows, the greater the shockwave when it inevitably bursts.

The British government established the South Sea Company in 1711 with a charter granting it an exclusive right to conduct trade with the Spanish colonies in the Americas. The prospects for this monopoly trade seemed, in principle, practically limitless, and the company, anticipating enormous future profits, agreed to buy up millions of pounds of government debt, providing its owners with a steady rate of interest income. To finance these debt purchases, company shares were sold to new investors on the London Stock Exchange. The Board of Governors deliberately talked up the price of these shares, tantalizing prospective investors with images of the vast riches to be made by a stake in the South Sea trade, even though scarcely a single company ship had yet sailed to the Americas.

By the spring of 1720, Britain was share-crazy. Everyone, from the highest ranks of the land to the lowest, seemed to be buying stock in the South Sea Company, often borrowing extravagantly to do so. The share price skyrocketed. From January to August, the price of a company share rose from £128 to more than £1,000. Hoping to cash in on the speculative mania, other entrepreneurs scrambled to sell shares in their business ventures too. Some of these were based on well-founded ideas, while others were ridiculously vague—one new public firm advertised itself as "a company for carrying out an undertaking of great advantage, but nobody [is] to know what it is."[1] It did not matter; everyone wanted to buy shares. By the end of the summer, the value of these companies bore no rational relationship to their likely profitability.

The original investors in the South Sea Company, suspecting that the bubble was on the verge of bursting, quietly began to sell their stock. Others followed. The share price stopped rising, hovered, dipped, then plummeted. On the evening of the meeting at the Merchant Tailors' Hall, a company share was worth £650. The following day, it was down to £540. By the end of the month, it could be had for £135. Entire fortunes were wiped out in a matter of weeks. Famous men were among the victims: The poet and dramatist John Gay was ruined and almost died from the stress. Others were luckier: George Handel, the composer, had cannily sold his shares at the peak of

This wood engraving from 1720 shows Change Alley, at the junction of Lombard Street and Cornhill, during the time of the South Sea Bubble scandal. Speculation in the South Sea Company's stock led to an economic bubble that financially ruined many investors.

the bubble and made a killing. The government feared rioting from mobs of bankrupted investors. Directors of the company could not venture out into the street for fear of being assaulted. The Irish author Jonathan Swift wrote a biting satire describing the fate of the broken, foolhardy speculators:

> Subscribers here by thousands float
> And jostle one another down;
> Each paddling in his leaky boat
> And here they fish for gold—and drown.[2]

There are two ways of looking at the "South Sea Bubble." On the one hand, it is a story of sheer recklessness, the gullibility of the greedy, and the callous unpredictability of the free market. On the other hand, it is also a demonstration of how economically dynamic Britain was at the beginning of the eighteenth century. There were failures and follies, to be sure, but the creation of an entrepreneurial culture, willing to invest in the future and take risks, was on balance a positive thing. Modern capitalism, with all its messy but vital energy, was being born.

Several things were going to be needed for the Industrial Revolution to take place in Great Britain. The first of these was excess capital, or money. Setting up an industrial business would be expensive: Grand schemes and enthusiasm were not enough. Machines, factory space, and raw materials all needed to be bought first. Entrepreneurs needed financiers willing to invest in their ideas. They would also need consumers, people willing to buy the new goods that would churn out of their workplaces. It was this radical transformation of business practices and domestic markets in late-seventeenth and early-eighteenth-century Britain that made the Industrial Revolution possible.

A "BUSINESS-FRIENDLY ENVIRONMENT"

In 1688, King James II was overthrown in a bloodless coup led by his Anglican Parliament, which was unhappy with the monarch's

Catholic beliefs. In his place, James's daughter, Mary, and her husband, the Dutch prince, William III, were invited to take the British throne. William only reigned for 13 years before meeting with an untimely demise: His horse stumbled into a mole's burrow, threw him, and he died from complications caused by a broken collarbone. But Britain's brief alliance with the Dutch monarchy had two important consequences for Britain's economic future. First, it helped to introduce new financial practices from Holland; and second, it dragged Britain into more than a century of warfare with France, which, despite the human and financial costs, ultimately proved to be a major boost for trade and industry.

At the end of the 1600s, Holland was at the leading edge of new innovations in finance. William's Dutch advisers brought to Britain imaginative new ideas about how the state should finance itself. Traditionally, the British government, like most European nations, had relied on coercion and crisis management to accrue funds. So-called tax farmers were empowered to threaten, cajole, and otherwise squeeze every penny they could from luckless taxpayers. Despite these efforts, there was never enough money to go around, so debt defaults were commonplace. For that reason, credit could only be obtained on very poor interest terms, which only made the system all the more unstable.

To alleviate this problem, the Bank of England was founded in 1694. The national bank loaned money to the government and in return was granted the right to sell stock and issue paper bills of exchange, or bank notes for gold or silver coins. This guaranteed the British state a secure, long-term, low-interest source of capital. At the same time, the revenue system was reformed. Tax farming was abolished, and a professional customs and excise service was created. Since they were now subject to predictable, rational taxation, businessmen could plan for the future with more confidence. The relationship between government and private enterprise changed, from one in which the state preyed arbitrarily on its subjects to one in which it encouraged and protected them. Britain was developing what would today be called a business-friendly environment.

Other financial innovations were developed in this period. In 1688, public offerings of joint-stock companies were sold and traded for the first time in London. The joint-stock company

ADAM SMITH (1723–1790)

Adam Smith was not someone you would call worldly. An unmarried man who lived alone with his mother, and seemed to inhabit a private existence of his own, he had long conversations with imaginary companions and was constantly beset with phantom illnesses. He had bulging eyes, a stammer, and a nervous twitch. His absentmindedness was notorious: On one occasion Smith was so engrossed in his own thoughts while on a tour of a leather-making factory that he fell head-first into a tanning pit. Yet this eccentric professor of moral philosophy dedicated much of his life to the study of that most worldly of pursuits: the art of making money. In *The Wealth of Nations*, published in 1776, he created the intellectual foundation for modern capitalism.

Smith was born in Kirkcaldy, a small town on the east coast of Scotland, in 1723; his father, a lawyer, had died six months earlier. When Smith was four, he was abducted by Gypsies and was only retrieved when a rescue party was sent to find him. At 14, he attended Glasgow University, later moving to England so he could study at Oxford. But he was unhappy away from home and had a nervous breakdown. After his recovery he made a living delivering public lectures in Edinburgh and was offered a professorship at Glasgow in 1751. In 1763, Smith took a new job as a private tutor to a young Scottish aristocrat and accompanied the youth on his travels across Europe, meeting such famous writers and thinkers as Benjamin Franklin and Voltaire. After three years, Smith returned to Scotland and spent the next decade writing allowed a large number of investors to pool their resources and share in business risk. That same year, Lloyd's of London began to offer insurance to ship owners; this was another key way of

a book, which encapsulated all his ideas about labor, trade, and the financial system.

The Wealth of Nations is one of the founding documents of modern economics and capitalism, although Smith never actually used those two words to describe his theory. One of his most important claims was that trade ought to be conducted between buyers and sellers without outside inter-ference: The most efficient transaction takes place if both parties are able to negotiate a mutually agreeable price influ-enced only by the natural laws of supply and demand—the price of an item rising when it is scarce and falling when it is abundant. Even though all the participants are seeking their own maximum self-interest, the overall result is beneficial to everyone. Smith called this benign outcome the result of an "invisible hand" leading everyone unwittingly to the best result for all.

It is true that, generally speaking, Smith believed that governments should keep taxation low and should avoid unnecessarily interfering with the operation of the free mar-ket through tariffs and other protectionist measures. But he did not believe that the free market model was appropriate to all economic activity. He supported the idea of state-funded education, government regulation of employment conditions like health and safety, and public investment in roads, bridges, and canals. Smith argued that a progressive income tax system (in which people pay a greater percentage of their income as they become wealthier) was fair. He even worried about the long-term environmental effects of industrial growth. Adam Smith was certainly a prophet of capitalism, but he was not unaware of the limitations of the system he advocated.

hedging risk and encouraging capital investment. The bills of exchange offered by the Bank of England increased the supply of money in circulation and hence the volume of trade, since it was no longer necessary to deal with gold and silver coins. Small commercial banks offering loans sprouted up across the country, promoting regional investment. A revolution in business information took place in thousands of coffeehouses across the nation, as potential investors gossiped and swapped stock tips.

Also in 1688, William III brought war to England, which proved to have economic benefits as well. William only accepted the British throne on condition that the country would immediately attack his greatest enemy, King Louis XIV of France. For the next 120 years, with only brief intervals, Britain was almost continuously in conflict with its neighbor across the English Channel. While war in Europe often dragged nations to economic ruin, Britain had one great advantage: Because it was an island state, its navy could protect it from invasion. There was no need to assemble a massive and often financially ruinous army. The British fought their war with France at a distance, attacking their enemy's rich overseas colonies and using part of the spoils to fund their allies on the continent. War acted as a financial bellows, encouraging the manufacture of ships and armaments. Investors grew rich on defense contracts. And those engines of war could be used to blockade French ports, shutting off France's exports while protecting Britain's. No wonder that Napoleon Bonaparte, exasperated by his inability to defeat his British enemies, would fume that England was a "nation of shopkeepers."[3]

THE CONSUMER SOCIETY

By the mid-1700s, Britain's overseas trade network, built up by war and investment, was the greatest in the world. But trade is only useful if there are customers, so the search for markets was keen. One important destination for British goods was its

The British fondness for tea grew tremendously during the Industrial Revolution, spurred on by trade with China. Seen here, a ceramic tea caddy decorated with caricatures of ladies' fashions, circa 1790 to 1800.

settlements in the Americas. From 1699 to 1774, exports to the 13 American colonies and Canada increased ninefold and what came to be known as the Atlantic system developed. British ships would sail to the coast of West Africa and trade cheap

"OF THE DIVISION OF LABOR"

One of Adam Smith's most revolutionary insights in his 1776 book, *The Wealth of Nations*, was his observation that work can be conducted more efficiently if it is broken down into a small number of simple tasks performed by many hands, rather than one highly skilled workman doing everything, a concept that underlies all modern industrial production. In the following extract, he looks at the way pins are made in England and suggests that this humble trade should act as the model for all future production in the country:

> To take an example from a very trifling manufacture; but one in which the division of labor has been very often taken notice of, the trade of the pin-maker; a workman not educated to this business (which the division of labor has rendered a distinct trade), nor acquainted with the use of the machinery employed in it (to the invention of which the same division of labor has probably given occasion), could scarce, perhaps, with his utmost industry, make one pin in a day, and certainly could not make twenty. But in the way in which this business is now carried on, not only the whole work is a peculiar trade, but it is divided into a number of branches, of which the greater part are likewise peculiar trades. One man draws out the wire, another straights it, a third cuts it, a fourth points it, a fifth grinds it at the top for receiving the head; to make the head requires two or three distinct operations; to

goods with the native populations in exchange for slaves. Those slaves would be transported, in atrocious conditions, to plantations in the Caribbean and in the southern American colonies, where they would be swapped for tobacco and cotton, which

put it on is a peculiar business, to whiten the pins is another; it is even a trade by itself to put them into the paper; and the important business of making a pin is, in this manner, divided into about eighteen distinct operations, which, in some manufactories, are all performed by distinct hands, though in others the same man will sometimes perform two or three of them.

I have seen a small manufactory of this kind where ten men only were employed, and where some of them consequently performed two or three distinct operations. But though they were very poor, and therefore but indifferently accommodated with the necessary machinery, they could, when they exerted themselves, make among them about twelve pounds of pins in a day. There are in a pound upwards of four thousand pins of a middling size. Those ten persons, therefore, could make among them upwards of forty-eight thousand pins in a day. Each person, therefore, making a tenth part of forty-eight thousand pins, might be considered as making four thousand eight hundred pins in a day. But if they had all wrought separately and independently, and without any of them having been educated to this peculiar business, they certainly could not each of them have made twenty, perhaps not one pin in a day; that is, certainly, not the two hundred and fortieth, perhaps not the four thousand eight hundredth part of what they are at present capable of performing, in consequence of a proper division and combination of their different operations. . . .*

---

*Adam Smith, *The Wealth of Nations* (1776). New York: Oxford University Press, 2008, pp. 12–13.

would be returned to Britain for resale. It was an enormously profitable, though inhumane, trade and was ultimately banned in Great Britain in 1807. But by that time Britain was able to pay for its raw material imports by selling finished manufactured goods to the Americans. Even the successful American Revolution against the British crown in the 1770s and early 1780s only briefly interfered with this trade; just a few years after the creation of the United States, Britain was sending more goods across the Atlantic than ever before.

The most important destination for British goods, however, was to be found at home. During the first half of the eighteenth century, the modern consumer market was created in Britain. The country's overall rise in prosperity gave millions of ordinary people some excess spending power for the first time. As class mobility increased, it became more and more important to demonstrate your social status by what you spent your money on rather than who your ancestors were.

In previous centuries, the demand for luxury goods had been confined almost exclusively to the rich and aristocratic. Now, relatively humble people were in the market for consumer goods too. Fashions, tastes, and fads began to proliferate, encouraged by the rise in literacy and the spread of newspapers and trade catalogs. Suddenly it became important to wear the latest colors and styles in clothes. A whole series of nationwide industries grew up to produce buttons, belts, hats, shoes, handkerchiefs, and gloves—accessories that would have been manufactured locally or not at all in earlier times. There was a particular craze for exotic imports such as Chinese silk and tea. The British obsession with tea drinking grew amazingly fast: The consumption of tea rose from virtually zero in the 1670s to 37 million pounds (16.7 million kg) by 1750. And of course tea parties needed crockery and cutlery; and furniture; and so on. Consumption fed on itself, the demand for one good creating a further demand for others. Money—and the urge to spend it—helped usher in the Industrial Revolution.

The Revolution in Farming

For almost all of the 400 years that followed the medieval "Black Death," or great bubonic plague, the population of Great Britain grew patchily or not at all. Then, at some point during the mid-eighteenth century, it began to rise—quickly. In 1700, about 5 million people were living in Britain. By 1800, that total had risen by more than half to 8 million. By the time of the Great Exhibition, in 1851, it had quadrupled to 20 million. It was the fastest rate of population growth in the world. The comparison with France, Britain's neighbor across the English Channel, is striking. At the beginning of the eighteenth century, France's population of 21 million dwarfed Britain's; two centuries later, Britain had overtaken France. And this rate of increase was taking place at the same

(continues on page 46)

THE MALTHUSIAN NIGHTMARE

In 1798, the Anglican cleric and political economist Thomas Malthus wrote an alarming commentary, his *Essay on the Principle of Population*, on the rapid population growth in Great Britain at the time. Malthus believed that, unless Britons had fewer children, the country would face mass starvation within a few generations. Malthus's dire prediction did not come true, because he underestimated the new productivity of Britain's farms thanks to the agricultural revolution. His essay, though, suggests how disconcerting the rise in Britain's population must have seemed to people at the beginning of industrialization:

> I think I may fairly make two [proposals]:
>   First, that food is necessary to the existence of man.
>   Secondly, that the passion between the sexes is necessary and will remain nearly in its present state. . . .
>   I say, that the power of population is indefinitely greater than the power in the earth to produce subsistence for man.
>   Population, when unchecked, increases in a geometrical ratio. Subsistence increases only in an arithmetical ratio. A slight acquaintance with numbers will show the immensity of the first power in comparison of the second. By that law of our nature which makes food necessary to the life of man, the effects of these two unequal powers must be kept equal.
>   This implies a strong and constantly operating check on population from the difficulty of subsistence. This difficulty must fall somewhere; and must necessarily be severely felt by a large portion of mankind.

Through the animal and vegetable kingdoms, nature has scattered the seeds of life abroad with the most profuse and liberal hand. She has been comparatively sparing in the room and the nourishment necessary to rear them. The germs of existence contained in this spot of earth, with ample food, and ample room to expand in, would fill millions of worlds in the course of a few thousand years. Necessity, that imperious all pervading law of nature, restrains them within the prescribed bounds. The race of plants, and the race of animals shrink under this great restrictive law. And the race of man cannot, by any efforts of reason, escape from it. Among plants and animals its effects are waste of seed, sickness, and premature death. Among mankind, misery and vice. The former, misery, is an absolutely necessary consequence of it. Vice is a highly probable consequence, and we therefore see it abundantly prevail; but it ought not, perhaps, to be called an absolutely necessary consequence. The ordeal of virtue is to resist all temptation to evil.

This natural inequality of the two powers of population, and of production in the earth, and that great law of our nature which must constantly keep their effects equal, form the great difficulty that to me appears insurmountable in the way to the perfectibility of society. . . . I see no way by which man can escape from the weight of this law which pervades all animated nature. No fancied equality, no agrarian regulations in their utmost extent, could remove the pressure of it even for a single century. And it appears, therefore, to be decisive against the possible existence of a society, all the members of which, should live in ease, happiness, and comparative leisure.*

---

* Thomas Malthus, *An Essay on the Principle of Population* (1798). New York: Oxford University Press, 2008, pp. 12-14.

(continued from page 43)

time that British people were emigrating in large numbers to the Americas and other parts of the colonial world. Quite suddenly, there were Britons everywhere.

Since there was no large-scale immigration into Britain at the time, the population could only have been rising for two reasons: either people were living longer or else they were marrying younger (and hence having more children). In fact, both of these phenomena were happening in Britain in the 1700s. Life expectancy had begun to increase. Someone born in England or Wales in the 1750s could expect to live to about 36 or 37. A century later, a newborn British baby's life expectancy was 40. During the same period, the average woman's age at marriage fell from 26 to 23. These changes may seem small, but over the course of time they made a huge difference to population size.

Why people were suddenly healthier, hardier, and more fertile is not really quite clear to historians, though there are a few suggestions. Improvements in the treatment of some killer diseases like smallpox may have helped. Because of the introduction of new foodstuffs, Britons probably had a more varied diet and better nutrition than before. The overall rise in prosperity probably encouraged young couples to marry earlier. But all this is speculation: What is known is that the population boomed.

In previous eras, this would not have provoked any great change in the economy. After all, every extra worker was also an extra mouth to feed. The new labor force would have consumed any additional food that was simultaneously produced at that time. But that is not what happened in Britain. At the same time that the overall size of the population grew, the share of the workforce in agriculture fell. By 1851, only one in five British adults worked on the land, the lowest proportion in the world. The new workers were being employed elsewhere—in urban factories. This transfer from the land to industry could only be achieved by a revolution in farming, one that was every bit as profound as the revolution that was soon to take place in manufacturing.

NEW METHODS IN AGRICULTURE

At the beginning of the 1700s, British farming practices were the same ones that had been used for 1,000 years; indeed, they had hardly changed since Roman times. Only very cautious and incremental improvements had been introduced during the Middle Ages. Plows had been given iron tips to better cut their way through the hard northern European soil. A rede-signed collar allowed oxen to be slowly replaced by horses, which lived longer and had greater endurance. The time in which fields had to lie unplanted, or "fallow," was reduced by farmers interspersing wheat and barley crops with an addi-tional "fodder crop" of oats that they could feed to their horses. Still, the output of each field, known as its yield, did not change much. In 1720, the typical British farmer only produced about 19 bushels of wheat for every acre (0.4 hectare).

Why farmers began to rethink their methods is a complex question, but part of the answer has to do with changes in the relationship between land ownership and the British state in the second half of the 1600s. Traditionally, all land in England and Wales had been held under feudal tenure, which meant that ultimate possession belonged to the king alone. Only he (and his government) could claim absolute rights over any piece of territory; the legal owner did not really own the land outright and could not simply sell or rent it to anyone he chose. When this feudal tenure system was abolished in 1660, land-owners were given much greater discretion to use their private property as they saw fit. Around the same time, the govern-ment began to rely more on excise taxes, rather than on land taxes, as its main source of revenue. Because landowners had to pay less to the state, they had more funds to invest; because they now owned the land outright, they had more incentive

(continues on page 50)

JETHRO TULL (1674–1741)

Jethro Tull grew up wanting to be a politician, not a farmer like his father, a Berkshire landowner. But bad health (he probably suffered from tuberculosis) and having to grapple with his family's many debts meant that, after attending St. John's College, Oxford, and seeking training as a lawyer in London, he was forced to return home to Berkshire to take up farming. There, his curiosity about new crop-growing techniques made him a pioneer in using technology to improve land productivity. He became one of the founding fathers of the British agricultural revolution.

Tull noticed that the traditional way of distributing crop seed on tilled ground, with workers scattering random handfuls of it as they walked up and down the furrows, was wasteful. In 1701, he designed a mechanical "seed drill," a kind of wagon that could be pulled by a horse and dropped seed onto the ground in straight lines at consistent intervals. Because the seed was distributed in an even way, none of it was wasted. In addition, another horse-drawn device, called a horse-hoe, could then be used to uproot all the weeds growing in between the seeds without harming them (previously, the only way to remove weeds had been to periodically take the field out of production). Despite the poor, chalky quality of the soil on Tull's Berkshire estate, he was able to use his technique to improve crop yield. In a book published in 1731, *Horse-Hoeing Husbandry*, he popularized his novel mechanical devices.

Not all of Tull's innovations were so fortunate. He was (wrongly) obsessed with the idea that manure was

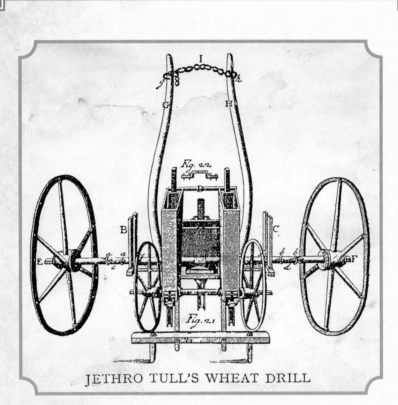

JETHRO TULL'S WHEAT DRILL

Jethro Tull invented the first seed drill circa 1701. Seed drills are sowing devices that position and cover seeds in the soil. Before invention of the seed drill, the common practice was to scatter seeds by hand.

useless as a crop fertilizer because seeds received all of the nutrition they needed from finely broken-up soil. This was a blind alley, although excusable perhaps given the very limited knowledge of plant physiology that existed in Britain in the early eighteenth century. Nonetheless, Tull's entrepreneurship and his determination to bring rational scientific methods to the previously haphazard craft of farming proved influential in the long run.

(continued from page 47)

to improve it. As the world of trade was being revolutionized in the late 1600s by new business ideas, farmers also began to think like modern capitalists and tried to increase profits by experimentation and entrepreneurship.

One of the most obvious new opportunities for growth was to reclaim wastelands like marshes, forests, and moors. By redeveloping these unused lands, the amount of arable soil under the plow increased by 30 percent from 1650 to 1800. But Britain remained a small island, and there was a definite fixed limit to the amount of new land that could be reclaimed. The only other way to increase profits was to increase yield on existing farmland—or in other words, to make farming more productive.

The breakthrough in productivity took place in the eastern county of Norfolk, and so became known as the Norfolk System. Norfolk farmers abandoned the old three-field crop rotation system of wheat-oats-fallow and introduced a four-field system of turnips-barley-clover-wheat. The fodder crops of turnip and clover, loaded with nitrogen, helped enrich the soil without the need to leave it fallow for part of every year. Farmers also added "marl," or clay, to the sandy Norfolk soil to oxygenate it and improve its drainage. By careful experimentation and observation, they produced remarkably high yields: Thirty years after 1730, total land value across the county had grown tenfold. By the 1840s, farmers using Norfolk System methods were averaging a yield of 30 bushels of wheat per acre (0.4 ha).

Elsewhere in Britain, farmers also began selective animal breeding, deliberately mating livestock to encourage the development of commercially desirable physical characteristics in their offspring. Robert Bakewell, a Lincolnshire landowner, pioneered the New Leicester sheep, which had delicate bones, a high-quality fleece, and most important of all, hefty forequarters—just the thing to satisfy the fashionable British taste for fatty shoulder mutton. Breeders like Bakewell literally changed the shape of the British farm animal. During the 1700s the weight of the typical sheep sold in London's markets doubled from 40 to 80 pounds (18 to 36 kg).

ENCLOSURE

But the biggest change of all, and the one that had the greatest consequence for the people of the British countryside, was the enclosure movement. Over the centuries, farms had developed in a haphazard, seemingly random way, known as the open field system. A great landowner's fields would be subdivided into many tiny plots, all different sizes and organized in no particularly logical way. Each plot would be tended by a single tenant family that had lived and worked there for generations, even centuries. This patchwork of small strips was broken up by swathes of "the commons," either woods or rough grazing land, which no single farmer owned. By ancient custom, all members of a local community had an equal right to use the commons to plant crops, collect firewood, hunt game, graze livestock, or even build houses. The poorer members of a village, with no land of their own, could eke out a modest but stable living on the commons.

Traditionally, most of the great landowners had tolerated this situation because that was the way it had always been. But as early as the sixteenth century, some of Britain's more ambitious farmers were unhappy with the irrationality of the open field system. It made no sense, they argued, for a valuable resource like land to be broken up into so many tiny and wasteful units. It would be far more efficient to consolidate, or "enclose," the land and organize it into larger and more uniform parts. But tenant farmers could not simply be evicted at will, even by the most powerful landlords. If their families had been there for many years, they had common law rights to continue their tenancies permanently. It would take an act of Parliament to repeal those rights and allow the landlords to remove them.

In 1727, the British government introduced the first of what would eventually be more than 4,000 enclosure acts, which

/ Draught and the Ufe of the several Sorts of Ploughs in England.

Engraved for the Univerfal Magazine for J. Hinton at the Kings Arms in St Pauls Church-Yard London. 1748.

Another boon to the British economy was the improvement of farming practices and tools during the Industrial Revolution. In this line engraving from 1748, draught horses and the use of several types of plows are depicted.

allowed landowners to reorganize their holdings, take over the commons as private property, and throw out unwanted tenants. By the mid-nineteenth century, more than 7 million acres (2.8 million ha)—two-thirds of all the arable land in Britain—had been affected by the enclosure movement. The landscape was permanently altered; rambling open fields stretching all the way to the horizon were replaced by a grid of much larger and tidier plots, each fenced off from the others by stone walls or thick hedgerows. The random patches of the commons disappeared, absorbed into the orderly pattern.

The response to enclosure by tenant farmers was mixed. Some, seeing crop prices fall and the value of their smallholding dwindle, agreed to sell out to the landowner peacefully. Others objected. Yet opposition to enclosure was not easy. It was possible to file a petition against a proposal to enclose land, but this required time, money, and familiarity with the law— all things that small farmers did not usually possess. In some cases, thanks to extraordinary efforts and the help of London lawyers, enclosure was postponed or prevented entirely. In most cases, though, the odds were stacked too high against the tenant. The biggest losers of all were the poorest members of the community who had scratched out a living on the fringes of the commons; they found themselves evicted and their homes demolished.

Looking back, there is a temptation to romanticize rural society before enclosure and to ignore the many practical benefits that land reform brought. That would be a mistake. Many small tenant farmers lived a meager, poverty-stricken existence, always one bad harvest away from starvation. Enclosure did prove to be far more efficient than the open field system, and the rise in food output ultimately made the cost of living cheaper for everyone. Nonetheless, to the bewildered tenant evicted from the home that he had been born and raised in, for no crime other than being on the losing side of history, enclosure seemed cruel and unnatural. An anonymous poet spoke of the seeming injustice of a system that appeared to favor only the rich and powerful:

> The fault is great in man or woman
> Who steals a goose from off a common;

But what can plead a man's excuse
Who steals a common from a goose?[1]

For many of these now-homeless former tenants, there was only one place to go. They drifted, inexorably, into the new industrial towns and cities to take their place on the factory floor.

The Textile Revolution

It was the night watchman who heard the shots first. The employees at William Cartwright's cotton mill in Rawfolds, Yorkshire, had been expecting an attack for several days; and on that Saturday night in April 1812, the firing of muskets to the north, south, east, and west meant that the attack was upon them. Within a few minutes, a group of armed men had rushed out of the darkness and overpowered the two guards posted at the mill gates. They began to smash the windows and pour musket shots into the factory. The mill's defenders responded with a volley of lead of their own; soon a full-scale firefight was taking place. Some defenders hidden on the roof unleashed a hail of stones upon their assailants. "Pull down the door!" and "Murder them!" were heard among the wretched screams of wounded men, but despite a number of desperate attempts to storm the building entrance, the attackers were forced back by the weight of fire.

After 90 minutes, the mob withdrew into the darkness, taking as many of their wounded as they could carry. Two men, Samuel Hartley and John Booth, injured so badly from musket balls that they could not walk, had to be left behind and died shortly after. Afterward, in an account of the attack published in a Yorkshire newspaper, one Cartwright mill defender wrote:

> We warn those that are engaged in these violent proceedings of the fatal consequences that await them in the unequal contest which they are now waging. . . . Let them reflect deeply on the fate [of] Hartley and Booth—let them recollect that they themselves may be the next victims, and let them stop in this desperate career before it is too late.[1]

In the spring of 1812, Great Britain was engaged in a full-scale war against Napoleon Bonaparte's French Empire. Rumors of a French invasion haunted the land. But the attack on the Rawfolds mill had nothing to do with power politics. It was one of the more violent skirmishes in a civil war taking place throughout the industrial north and Midlands of England, a fight not over the affairs of kings, but rather a struggle between the factory owners of the Industrial Revolution and the workers in traditional tradecrafts who felt that mechanization and mass production were destroying their livelihoods. Led by a mysterious (and probably mythical) rabble-rouser called Ned Ludd, these "Luddites," as they were known, assembled in secret societies and led raids on mills and textile factories, smashing up work spaces and wrecking machines. In response, industrialists armed their employees and appealed to London for assistance. Alarmed at this homegrown insurrection at a time of war, the British government sent in 12,000 troops and made "machine breaking" a crime punishable by hanging. Fourteen men were executed for participation in the attack in Rawfolds.

Luddites were British textile artisans who feared that their jobs would be lost to mechanized looms. In this illustration, Luddites smash looms in a factory during the riots of 1811 to 1816.

Others were transported as convicts to the British penal colony in Australia.

Luddism was a desperate response by some otherwise law-abiding people to the dramatic changes taking place in the British textile industry at the dawn of the nineteenth century. The introduction of new machinery and the reorganization of how work was performed through the factory system brought great improvements in efficiency, driving up production rates and lowering costs. The revolution in the cotton trade, in particular, would act as a model for all future industrialization. These changes would, at least in the long term, raise the standard of living for ordinary workers in industrial towns and cities. But their immediate effects were often brutal. Men were frequently thrown out of their jobs, and the traditional ways of life in tight-knit communities were dismantled. The Luddite revolt is a stark illustration of just how bewildering and unjust the advance of industrialization could seem to those who lived through it.

THE RISE OF "KING COTTON"

At the dawn of the Industrial Revolution, the woolen trade dominated Britain's textile industry. Raw materials were easy to obtain: The country had an abundance of sheep farms. During the Middle Ages, this wool was exported to Flanders (modern Belgium) for "finishing," or turning into manufactured goods like clothing, but by 1700, some entrepreneurs in northern English towns like Leeds had begun finishing it themselves. The domestic woolen trade was given some helpful protection by laws that required, for instance, all burial shrouds to be made of wool. As the amount of capital available for investment grew, so the woolen trade expanded. Between the 1720s and the 1740s, the annual amount of finished woolen goods produced in Leeds doubled.

Despite its usefulness and popularity, wool was not the ideal material for mass production. It was too fragile and uneven to be easily worked by machines. Cotton offered far greater possibilities. It was not, however, a plant grown in Britain—it had to be imported from the Middle East, and later from the United States—but from the point of view of manufacturers, cotton goods had a number of advantages over woolen ones. Cotton, a much more durable and uniform material, could withstand rough treatment from machinery. It also appealed to the growing consumer taste for new styles in clothing. Cotton clothes were lighter, longer lasting, and could be more easily

During the Industrial Revolution, the manufacture of cotton goods was improved through the development of a series of efficient mechanical looms. One of the major improvements was the invention of the water frame by Richard Arkwright, a type of spinning frame driven by waterpower.

washed. They could be dyed with more vibrant colors. Most importantly, the appeal of cotton was worldwide. British manufacturers had always had a hard time selling woolen goods to warm tropical markets. Cotton could be worn by all customers, wherever they lived. The cotton trade would turn out to be the business perfectly suited to early industrialization; it propelled British economic development in the late 1700s just as the digital industry would transform the U.S. economy two centuries later.

To make cotton goods, four steps were involved. The cotton first had to be cleaned of dirt and seeds, and "combed," or straightened out; second, it had to be spun, to turn it into

RICHARD ARKWRIGHT (1733–1792)

Richard Arkwright was not an easy man to get along with. He was stubborn and argumentative, and ended his life estranged from most of his family; he had furious rows with colleagues and was accused of illegally copying his inventions from others. The writer Thomas Carlyle described him as "gross, bag-cheeked, and potbellied."* Yet his noncompliant personality was part of what made him a business success. One of the first self-made men of the Industrial Revolution, he rose from poverty to become fabulously rich and influential, guided by nothing other than hard work, acute business insight, and a sometimes ruthless willingness to seize the new opportunities offered up by changing economic times. He was a model of the new industrial titan.

The youngest of a family of 13, Arkwright was born in Preston, Lancashire, in 1733. His father, a tailor, was too poor to send him to school, and his cousin taught him to read and write. He was apprenticed to a barber and wigmaker in the nearby town of Bolton, where Arkwright learned his first trade, eventually taking over a small barbershop himself. His thoughts, however, were already turning to the growing Lancashire cotton trade. Aware of the demand for a new spinning process to accelerate the production of cotton, he and a local clockmaker named John Kay came up with a prototype device that could spin cotton faster. It was patented in 1769 and dubbed the "water frame."

a fine thread; third, it had to be woven into cloth; and finally, the cloth had to be bleached or printed. Each step involved different skills and different technological challenges. As each

Two years later Arkwright managed to get enough financial backing to open up a mechanized cotton mill of his own. He and his partners spent more than £12,000 on capital investment in the mill, a fantastic sum of money in the 1770s, but the gamble worked. After paying off his fellow investors, Arkwright expanded his own manufacturing business and also used his patent to sell water frames to other entrepreneurs. By the mid-1780s, about 30,000 people worked in factories using Arkwright machinery. He was distracted for many years by a series of drawn-out legal challenges from John Kay and other early collaborators, who claimed that their ideas had been stolen; Arkwright ultimately lost many of his patents, but by that point they had made him rich. With money also came social respectability. He was knighted in 1786 and became the high sheriff of the county of Derbyshire.

Part of Arkwright's success—and much of his notoriety—lay in the strict discipline he demanded of his employees. Millworkers at an Arkwright factory had to present themselves at the gates at precise times of the day and could be fined for even the slightest lateness or infraction. He employed children as young as seven for long hours and low wages. Not all of his innovations were harsh, however. Arkwright gave his employees holidays and provided them with elementary education. Though a severe taskmaster, he accepted that he had some paternal responsibilities toward his workers and offered them rudimentary benefits as long as they remained hardworking and loyal.

* Thomas Carlyle, *Chartism, Past and Present*. London: Chapman and Hall, 1858, p. 51.

step was simplified and sped up by machinery, it created an incentive to mechanize the others so as to keep up the total rate of production.

In 1733, the "flying shuttle" loom was invented, making the weaving process faster. This then increased the demand for thread, and the response in 1764 was the "spinning jenny," which allowed a single operator to spin eight threads at once. The spinning jenny, however, was soon replaced by the even more efficient "water frame" invented by the mill owner Richard Arkwright, until it in turn was made obsolete in 1779 by the "spinning mule," a composite of the first two devices. Spurred on by this ingenuity, the other steps in the cotton cycle also became faster: A "carding machine" made the combing process more efficient, and the finishing stage was revolutionized by a device that printed cloth using engraved copper cylinders. In 1785, the clergyman and amateur inventor Edmund Cartwright took the process to its logical conclusion when he harnessed a flying shuttle to one of the new steam engines being produced by James Watt. Soon all the steps in cotton manufacture had been vastly accelerated by steam power.

The impact of mechanization on the cotton trade can scarcely be exaggerated. In 1760, Britain imported 2.5 million pounds (1,133,980.925 kg) of raw cotton. By the 1830s, it was importing 366 million (166,014,807.42 kg) pounds annually. Cotton had replaced wool as the country's chief export, and the cotton trade accounted for fully 5 percent of national income. Traditional cotton manufacturers elsewhere in the world, such as India, were wiped out by the low price and volume of British cotton goods. King Cotton, with his more than 2,000 smoky factories scattered across industrial Britain, was victorious.

THE FACTORY SYSTEM

At the outset of the Industrial Revolution, the modern factory as we know it today did not exist. Manufacturing was entirely decentralized. Ironware, glassware, barrels, leather goods, and other important commodities were made in small workshops each run by a master, who employed a handful of journeymen who in turn trained a number of young apprentices. To become a journeyman, and perhaps eventually a master, apprenticeships were long and involved. It was necessary to learn every step in the manufacturing process, an education that took years. There was always a small supply of skilled employees, and so members of the trade enjoyed job security.

In a similar way, textile merchants sent out small amounts of raw wool or cotton to be combed, spun, and woven in private households in the countryside. Working in their cottages (which gave us the term *cottage industry*), these textile workers—often farmworkers' wives or daughters—supplemented the family income with their part-time employment. During the early stages of wool and cotton industrialization, the scale of this "domestic system," as it was known, grew rapidly. Hand spinners and hand weavers prospered as the demand for textiles skyrocketed.

A number of forward-thinking entrepreneurs, like Richard Arkwright, believed that there would be great advantages to consolidating manufacturing in a single place. Expensive machines such as the flying shuttle loom and the spinning mule had to be physically located and operated in one location. Rather than send out the work to the employees, why not send the employees to the work? Great efficiencies could also be introduced by specializing labor. In *The Wealth of Nations*, Adam Smith had noted that the manufacture of goods such as pins could be made much faster if a small number of skilled workers making the pin from scratch were replaced by a chain of unskilled workers performing just one single repetitive task as part of the overall process. Not only was this more efficient, but these easily

(continues on page 66)

LIFE FOR CHILDREN IN THE NEW FACTORIES

Although the textile factories of the industrial north and Midlands, equipped as they were with the latest weaving technology, produced huge profits for their owners and for the nation, their employees suffered enormously. In 1833, a Parliamentary Select Committee that was considering reform of working conditions for factory laborers interviewed many people who had experienced life in these mills. One such witness was Samuel Coulson. His testimony is excerpted here:

Have you any family?
Yes.

Have any of them worked in a mill?
Yes, three daughters.

At what age did they begin to work?
The elder was going 12, and the middlemost going 11 and the youngest going 8 when they went to the mill first; they are older now.

At what time in the morning, in the brisk time, did those girls go to the mills?
In the brisk time, for about six weeks, they have gone at 3 o'clock in the morning and ended at 10 or nearly half past at night. . . .

What intervals were allowed for rest or refreshment during those 19 hours of labour?
Breakfast a quarter of an hour, and dinner half an hour, and drinking a quarter of an hour. . . .

Was any of that time taken up in cleaning the machinery?
They generally had to do what they call drying down; sometimes this took the whole of the time at breakfast or

drinking, and they were to get their dinner or breakfast as they could; if not, it was brought home.

Sometimes they could not get their breakfast at all?
Sometimes they could not. . . .

Had you not great difficulty in awakening your children to this excessive labour?
Yes, in the early time we had them to take up asleep and shake them, when we got them on the floor to dress them, before we could get them off to their work, but not so in the common hours.

What were the common hours?
Six o'clock in the morning till half past eight at night. . . .

What was the length of time they could be in bed during those long hours?
It was near 11 o'clock before we could get them into bed after getting a little victuals, and then at morning my mistress [wife] used to stop up all night, for fear that we could not get them ready for the time: sometimes we have gone to bed, and one of us generally woke up.

What time did you get them up in the morning?
In general me or my mistress got up at 2 o'clock to dress them.

So that they had not above 4 hours sleep at this time?
No, they had not. . . .

Were the children excessively fatigued by this labour?
Many times; we have cried often when we have given them the little [food] we had to give them; we had to shake them, and they have fallen to sleep with the food in their mouths many a time. . . . *

---

* "Minutes of the Evidence taken before the Committee on the Factories" (1833). http://www.historyhome.co.uk/peel/factmine/coulson.htm.

(continued from page 63)

trained workers could be paid much less and replaced much more quickly—something that did not escape the attention of men like Arkwright.

By the late 1700s, such "manufactories"—eventually shortened to just "factories"—were being built across northern and midland England. They tended to be placed near rivers or canals, because these waterways provided a source of power (through waterwheels) and because the transport of goods was still much cheaper by boat than by road. As workers migrated toward factories, villages, and later towns, grew up around them. Manchester, in many ways the archetypal factory town, grew from 25,000 inhabitants in 1777 to more than 300,000 by 1851. Early textile factories, however, were nothing like the size of later industrial plants; most had fewer than 50 employees. Nonetheless, the shift toward factory production in eighteenth-century Britain was a major step in the transformation of working life in the modern world.

Factory employees ultimately shared in some of the profits of their work and their standard of living improved, albeit slowly. The annual wage of a factory worker had risen from about £25 in 1750 to roughly £44 in 1860. But many masters and journeymen were thrown out of work, their hard-won skills made obsolete by machinery. Moreover, even those who benefited financially from the factory saw their lives reorganized in ways that were distressing. Factory owners demanded strict timekeeping and a disciplined work environment. People who had been used to working to their own schedule and within the familiar confines of their own household now found themselves performing monotonous tasks for hours on end, barked at by overseers who demanded faster production rates. Children and women, who were more pliable and could be paid less, were crowded into dirty, unsafe, and unsanitary buildings in which they froze in winter and baked in summer. Until legal reforms regulating factory conditions were introduced in the early nineteenth century, there was little that ordinary workers could do about their situation. No wonder, then, that the English poet William Blake would refer to these new smoky brick edifices on the landscape as England's "dark satanic mills."[2]

The Age of
Iron and Steam

No one would have called the *Rocket* beautiful. She was not a sleek sailing ship or a graceful riding buggy. A rickety contraption of iron, copper, and wood, with pipes and cylinders at odd angles and a huge ungainly smokestack belching black fumes, she looked like a great metal barrel mounted on a stagecoach. Yet this clumsy monster puffing her way up the track on the morning of September 15, 1830, was the flag bearer of a revolution in transportation, inaugurating the modern age of travel and communications. For on this day, the world's first railroad to transport passengers and goods was opening, and people would never experience space and time in quite the same way again.

The Rocket was the prizewinning entry in a competition staged the previous year to pull the first carriages along the newly built railroad from Liverpool to Manchester. Both cities in the

The remains of Robert Stephenson's *Rocket* are seen here on display. It was an early steam locomotive built at the Forth Street Works in Newcastle upon Tyne in 1829.

north of England were pivotal to the Industrial Revolution: Manchester, the seat of King Cotton, was the center of the massive Lancashire textile trade, and Liverpool, the great northwestern port of England, was the gateway to the world's oceans. With just 35 miles (56 km) separating the two cities, the economic link between them was vital: Manchester mill owners needed to get raw cotton unloaded and shipped to them from the Liverpool docks and finished cotton cloth returned back to Liverpool for overseas export. Time was

GEORGE STEPHENSON (1781–1848)

George Stephenson was one of those men whose rags-to-riches story epitomizes the social changes brought about by industrialization. Born the son of a colliery fireman in a humble cottage a few miles outside Newcastle in 1781, young George tended sheep and had no formal education. At an earlier point in British history, his talents would almost certainly have gone unrecognized and unrewarded. Yet when Stephenson died in 1848, having made his name synonymous with the railroad, he was a rich and celebrated man, having twice turned down the offer of a knighthood. In every sense, his life was bound up with the challenges and opportunities of the Industrial Revolution.

While working as a junior engineer at his father's mine, Stephenson attended night school to learn to read and write. He never possessed any great scientific knowledge (his son Robert would later assist him in technical matters), but he became an acute observer of machinery by trial-and-error experiments. He spent his leisure hours at money: All of this needed to happen as quickly and cheaply as possible. But the existing road and canal network was much too expensive and inefficient. So industrialists had pooled their capital to invest in a bold and pioneering project: a railroad line between Liverpool and Manchester, with the wagons pulled by a steam locomotive.

It was not a simple task. The distance was short, but the geography complicated. Several hills, too steep to be climbed by the primitive locomotives available at the time, would have to be

the mine tinkering with Newcomen and Boulton-Watt steam engines, learning how they worked and how they might be improved. In 1814, the mine owners gave Stephenson permission to design a steam locomotive (the first, constructed by Richard Trevithick, was built in Wales in 1804), and his design proved so promising that he was contracted to build an eight-mile (12.8-km) railroad to run it on. One of Stephenson's insights was that, in order to get maximum efficiency from the primitive locomotives of his day, railroads needed to be as flat and straight as possible; train engineers also needed the skills of surveying, bridge-, and tunnel-building. His pioneer projects got him the contract to design a locomotive track from Stockton to Darlington. In 1829, he won his most famous commission of all: the building of the Liverpool to Manchester railroad, on which his own train, the *Rocket*, would run.

Stephenson was kept busy for the remainder of his life on track and train construction. Many of the first locomotives used in the United States came from his engine workshops. The ultimate testament to his craft is that many of the bridges, viaducts, and track foundations he created almost 200 years ago remain in use to this day.

burrowed through. A long valley at Sankey Brook would have to be crossed somehow. And then there was Chat Moss, a peat bog lying right across the path of the line. Its marshy ground was so soft that a train would sink right into it. George Stephenson— the inventor of the *Rocket* and also an accomplished civil engineer who had built the *Locomotion*, the first public steam railway in the world, for the Stockton and Darlington Railway in northeast England in 1825—was given the project.

Stephenson made his calculations. In all, 64 bridges and viaducts would be needed. In this era before modern mechanical digging and construction equipment, thousands of laborers, known as "navigators" or "navvies" for short, were contracted to build the railroad line using only shovels, pickaxes, and muscle power. Under Stephenson's direction, the navvies bored 70 feet (21 m) into solid rock for 2 miles (3.2 km). They dug a 2,250-yard (2,057-m) tunnel under Liverpool itself. They bridged Sankey Brook with a 70-foot-high (21-m-high) viaduct. At Chat Moss, they spent weeks painstakingly laying a stone, earth, and wood foundation for the railroad tracks. It was a triumph of sheer willpower and a testament to the "can-do" attitude of Britain during the Industrial Revolution.

The railroad was a magnificent success. Soon thousands of tons of raw cotton and cloth were rolling back and forth between Liverpool and Manchester at 17 miles (27 km) per hour—not terribly impressive by modern standards perhaps, but revolutionary in the 1830s. In 1831, the railroad's owners made a profit of more than £136,000, an enormous sum for the era. Moreover, more than 400,000 people traveled as passengers between the two cities, many leaving their hometowns for the first time in their lives. The prosperity of the Liverpool and Manchester line sparked a boom in railroad building in Britain and in the United States that would last for the next century.

The *Rocket* was the logical culmination of two connected revolutions: one of technology, the other of communications.

During the preceding century, the British iron and coal industries had expanded many times over, with the steam engine, a new and dynamic source of power, propelling the expansion of both. At the same time, entrepreneurs had striven to improve internal transport routes throughout Britain, as the booming economy demanded the unprecedented movement of goods and people. Mounting a steam engine on iron rails to create a locomotive was the nineteenth century's ultimate solution to this problem. It was an answer that would not only bring enormous profits but would also (almost by accident) change ordinary life and create the modern nation-state.

IRON, COAL, AND STEAM

Cotton was one of the materials that made the Industrial Revolution; iron was another. As manufacturing output increased in the new workplaces of early commercial England, so the importance of iron grew: iron for machinery; iron for consumer products like cookware and tools; iron for the cannons of the British Army and Navy. Because of this, the country found itself increasingly reliant on imports of iron from countries like Sweden and Russia. The problem was not a lack of iron ore. The problem was that iron ore had to be "smelted," or heated in an intense furnace, to extract the usable iron; and the only way of doing this in the early 1700s was by the use of charcoal, derived from wood. Britain's great medieval forests, however, were long gone, and there simply was no longer a big enough source of timber.

What Britain did have in abundance, however, was coal. The country sat on the vast northwestern European coal seam that stretches from Wales through Belgium into Germany. In 1709, Abraham Darby, a Bristol manufacturer, figured out a way of smelting iron using "coke," an extract of coal, setting off a series of technological improvements in the size and efficiency of blast furnaces. With the fuel problem resolved and the procedure for smelting much simplified and cheapened, Britain switched from being a net iron importer into the world's biggest iron exporter. In 1720, the country produced 25,000 tons (22,679 metric tons) of pig iron a year. By 1804, 10 times as much were made.

This, however, put pressure on the coal industry to increase its output. And as mines got larger and broke through the water table deep underground, the problem of flooding became severe. A method had to be devised to remove water from mine shafts faster than humans or animals could do it. The breakthrough in this case was made by Thomas Newcomen, an ironmonger and Baptist lay preacher who lived in Devon, a county in southwestern England with a long history of tin mining. Newcomen's idea was to use steam power to drive a mechanical pump. He built a large copper kettle in which water was heated to the boiling point. The steam pressure pushed up a piston mounted in a cylinder above the kettle. Cold water was allowed to enter the cylinder, condensing the steam; this created a vacuum that drew the piston downward. Then the process was repeated. The continual up-and-down motion of the piston could be used to work a pump. Newcomen's steam engine produced far more power than traditional pumping; in two days it could do a week's worth of work by 50 men and 20 horses.

The relationship between iron, coal, and steam would be a dynamic one. The more steam engines were built, the more iron was needed; the more iron smelted, the more coal was needed; the more coal mined, the more steam engines were needed to pump water. And so on . . .

THE TRANSPORTATION REVOLUTION

The British faced a paradoxical transportation situation at the beginning of the eighteenth century. Advances in navigation and shipbuilding over the preceding centuries had allowed European travelers and merchants to sail across the world, exploring and trading. By the dawn of the Industrial Revolution, it was commonplace for British vessels to ship goods and people thousands of miles to the Americas, Africa, and Asia. Yet it was almost as hard to send a consignment of goods from one town to the next as it was to send them across an ocean. Internal transportation within Britain itself was no better than it had been 1,000 years earlier. If anything, it was worse. Trains of pack-mules had to negotiate muddy tracks that had not been properly repaired since Roman times. These conditions presented an enormous handicap to industrialists. It was all very well to have the means to ship raw cotton from Virginia or Egypt to Liverpool, but what if the cotton then had to sit in quayside warehouses rotting away because of the inability to transport it to the Lancashire mills just 30 miles (48 km) to the east? Entrepreneurs realized that, before they could properly exploit their new advances in technology and organization, they would have to fix Britain's broken transport network.

First, the roads needed mending. The solution was the creation of "turnpike trusts," which were cooperative businesses set up by landowners and industrialists who pooled their money to rebuild the ancient road networks. By law they were allowed to collect tolls along the roadway, which helped to pay for the reconstruction and maintenance. A major problem was that horse-drawn carts and wagons created ruts in the road surface, which then developed into potholes that became flooded in wet weather. Two Scotsmen, Thomas Telford and John McAdam, came up with methods of creating solid road bases that drained off rainwater and kept the surface dry, flat, and firm. With long-term investment in the roadways, land transportation became much faster. In 1745, it still took two weeks to travel from London to Edinburgh, but 50 years later that journey had been reduced to three days. Stagecoach travel, which had previously been irregular and expensive, became cheaper and more reliable.

The roads alone, however, could not keep up with the demand for the shipment of goods. So the industrialists also turned to internal water transport: canals. Unlike rivers, which meandered across the landscape and did not always take boats where they were most needed, artificial canals could be dug straight and custom-engineered to link vital economic centers. Canal technology had been familiar for centuries, but the construction of a major canal system required an enormous capital investment. Before industrialization there had never been enough cargo to justify such a grand expense. The expansion of the coal, iron, and textile trades was the catalyst necessary for change.

The construction of the Bridgewater Canal in 1761 was illustrative of the new thinking. The Duke of Bridgewater needed to get coal from his mines to the iron foundries in Manchester 10 miles (16 km) away. He contracted a young engineer, James Brindley, to design and build a canal for him. The sums involved were vast—£168,000—but upon completion, Brindley's canal cut the cost of shipping coal to Manchester in half. While it had previously taken 8 horses to haul a 6-and-a-half-ton (5.8 metric tons) wagon, now a single horse walking along a canal towpath could pull a barge weighing 30 tons (27.2 metric tons). "Canal mania" soon swept Britain; by 1800, 1,400 miles (2,253 km) of canals had been constructed across the land.

Yet even the new canals were not enough to keep up with the expansion in trade. The steam engine pointed to a final solution: the automation of goods transportation by iron railroad. George Stephenson's completion in 1825 of a 26-mile (42-km) rail line running from the northeastern coal town of Darlington to the port of Stockton demonstrated the future of railroad technology. With the success of Stephenson's much more ambitious Liverpool to Manchester line five years later, Britain was swept up in "railroad mania" just as it had been with canal mania a half-century before. By 1851, 6,800 miles (10,944 km) of track were laid across the country, linking every major town and industrial region. More than 30 million passengers a year were traveling by railroad also.

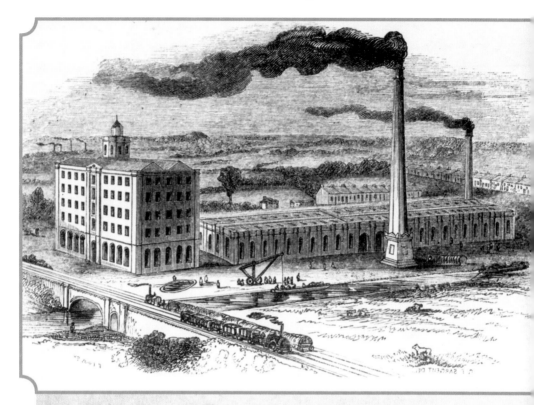

In this circa-1840 illustration, the Bridgewater Foundry situated by the Bridgewater Canal is shown. In order to move goods more efficiently through Great Britain and out across the world, canals were cut all through the British Isles during the Industrial Revolution.

Of all the transportation innovations of the Industrial Revolution, the railroad was the most life changing—and the most controversial. Critics warned that these strange new machines were unsafe (it did not help that a man was crushed to death on the opening day of the Liverpool to Manchester line) and that passengers would asphyxiate in their carriages. Locomotives would ruin crops, spoil milk, and kill birds. Yet the appeal of railroad travel was unquenchable. No one had ever experienced the sensation of such high-speed motion before. Moreover, the railroad brought the possibility of movement and change to millions of ordinary people. Where once it had been far too expensive to travel from one part of the country to another unless absolutely necessary, now passengers could explore hundreds of miles at will. Men and

THE FIRST RAILROAD DEATH

The opening of the Liverpool to Manchester railroad on September 15, 1830, was not just a milestone in the history of transportation; it was also the site of the world's first fatal railroad accident. The unfortunate man who would go down in history as the first person killed by a train was William Huskisson, an important member of Parliament for Liverpool. Years later, Dr. J.P. Brandreth, who had also been a passenger on the railroad that day and who attended to Huskisson after the accident, wrote an account of the incident:

> I was on the last seat of the first train, fellowed by six other steam engines, containing near 300 persons. The Duke of Wellington's carriage was on the other line—i.e., the south—and several times passed us at great speed, and then, stopping, allowed us to pass him. On our arrival at Parkside, 17 miles [27.3 km] from Liverpool, which had been accomplished in 55 minutes, the duke's carriage, with about 70 persons, was taking water, and we passed on to our watering-place, about half a mile in advance, and, per-ceiving that the other trains were considerably behind us, I got on top of the cutting to look back for them. I saw two trains arrive, and stop at their purpose place, but observ-ing that the fourth remained opposite the duke's carriage, a quarter of a mile short of where it ought to have been, I was fearful some accident had happened, and immediately walked down towards it. I was soon met by Mr. Forsyth, almost exhausted by running, who was coming for me, in consequence of Mr. Huskisson having been run over.

women from one part of Britain regularly mingled with those from another for the first time and got to know and understand one another. In this way the railroad did more than

I hurried and found Mr. Huskisson on a door lying on the railway, Lord Wilton having twisted a handkerchief round the thigh. . . . We placed him in the car occupied by the band and set off to Manchester. In a few minutes he became so faint that I stopped the engine to inquire if any bleeding had taken place; and determined them to remain at the first house we came to, conceiving his speedy dissolution to be inevitable. . . . It occurred to me that we might stop at Mr. Blackburne's at Eccles. . . . When I mentioned this arrangement to him he appeared much pleased and said, "Pray do so; I am sure my friend Mr. Blackburne will be kind to me." . . .

[At the house] he had some laudanum and ether administered. . . . I cut the boot and clothes off the wounded leg and placed him in the drawing-room upon a low half sofa. . . . The leg presented a frightful appearance . . . half way between the knee and ankle was almost entirely severed, except a small portion on the outside, but the boot was scarcely marked at all. Half-way but rather higher up between the knee and body, the whole flesh was torn off above the bones broken. . . . [Mr. Huskisson] retained his self-possession throughout. . . . To myself he said, "You see I shall never live to make any return for your kindness. You have done all that was possible but it is in vain. Why endeavor to support my strength? I must die: It is only prolonging my sufferings."

He died at twenty minutes past nine, I believe, without much interval of relief. . . .*

* "First Railway Accident," *Liverpool Mercury*, 1913. http://www.old-merseytimes.co.uk/huskisson.html.

just make the transport of goods more convenient; it also helped to bridge geographical differences and suspicions. In an important way, trains created a sense of national identity in Britain and would later do the same in Europe and the United States.

The Rise of
the Industrial City

On Sunday, February 12, 1832, Sarah Ferguson was brought into Limehouse Workhouse hospital, complaining of cramps and vomiting. Within eight hours the normally healthy woman, who made a living scavenging coal and pieces of wood along the mud-banks of the River Thames, was dead. Shortly before her demise, her arms and legs turned a deep blue color. This confirmed her doctor's worst fears: She was north London's first victim of the worldwide cholera outbreak. Cholera—a bacterial infection of the small intestines—had already killed millions in China and India and had been slowly spreading westward for the previous two years, drifting along the trade routes back to Europe. Some outbreaks had been reported in Edinburgh and Newcastle, and Londoners had waited in fear. Any hopes that Sarah Ferguson's death would be an isolated incident were quickly dashed when a mother and daughter, Mary and Caroline Sheah, also fell ill and died within hours. The three were hastily buried in deep graves in a local church-yard. But by then the news had gotten out, and London was in panic. "King Cholera" was on the rampage.

Cholera was the most dreaded of all diseases because of its speed and lethality. At the time, no one understood why it spread; all that was known for sure was that the blueing of the skin almost certainly meant death within a few hours. Unlike

JOHN SNOW (1813–1858)

John Snow was an example of an underprivileged boy who rose through education and hard work to become a member of Britain's prosperous nineteenth-century middle class. Yet unlike some of his peers, he never lost his sense of duty to those less fortunate than himself. Snow's dedication was ultimately decisive in combating the deadliest illness of the industrial era, cholera, for it was his path-breaking observations that proved once and for all that the disease was spread by contaminated water and not by "bad air" or some of the other theories popular at the time.

Snow was born into a poor family in a slum district of York, in northern England. His father was a laborer and later a farmer, but thanks to family connections, he was able to secure a good education for his son. The boy was eventually apprenticed to a doctor. During the 1832 cholera outbreak, a young Snow helped to treat convalescing miners at Yorkshire collieries, his first direct encounter with the disease.

After setting up a general practice in London in 1838, he received training in surgery and became interested in the new science of anesthetics that was developing in the other diseases, cholera seemed to be indifferent to class and status. Everyone, rich and poor alike, was vulnerable to it. Soon every cough, sneeze, and minor ailment was being taken as a sign of cholera. Normal life in London broke down. The only treatments available for victims were medical guesswork: blankets, hot baths, brandy, and laudanum (opium) to ease the passage into death. Wild rumors flared. Some Londoners insisted that cholera was spread by political agitators, or pharmacists out to profit from sales of medicine. Reactions among the country's

city's hospitals. His experimentation with chloroform—a gas that allowed patients to undergo surgery without fear of pain—was so successful that he was asked to administer it to Queen Victoria when she had her last two children. Snow's successful treatment of the queen established his reputation.

It was his investigative work during the 1854 cholera outbreak in central London, however, that was to be his permanent legacy. Cholera had already hit other areas of the capital the previous year, but the epidemic that broke out in Broad Street, near Soho, was the most devastating yet: 127 people died in three days. By exhaustively interviewing as many local residents as possible and using statistical methods, Snow was able to demonstrate that the source of the Broad Street outbreak was a single water pump: Almost all the deaths had occurred in a cluster of houses surrounding it. Excavation later showed that a nearby cesspit had contaminated the well from which the water was pumped. Snow's work did not provide a cure for cholera: A full understanding of and treatment for the disease would not be available until the discovery of germs in the 1880s. But by pinning down the cause of cholera epidemics, Snow made a direct link between public health and good urban sewage treatment and clean water supplies.

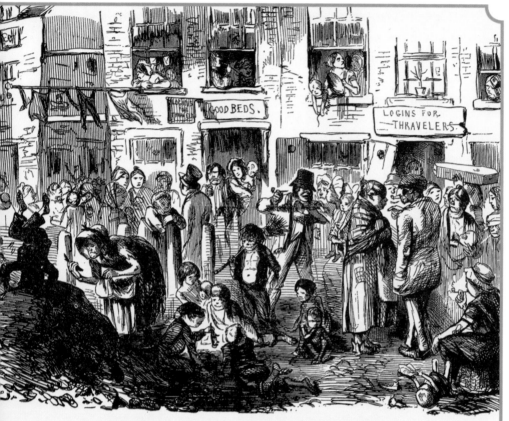

A COURT FOR KING CHOLERA.

Cholera spread like wildfire through the poorer sections of industrial cities in the nineteenth century. After a vicious outbreak in 1832, "King Cholera" continued to break out across Great Britain over the next 20 years. In this September 1852 cartoon from *Punch*, poor children play in piles of garbage. The following year cholera was epidemic in London.

wealthiest varied. Some philanthropists set up soup kitchens and handed out clothes to the poorest of London's underclass, who were made destitute during the epidemic with the closure of factories and workplaces. Others, however, insisted that helping the poor would only make them breed faster, and so it was kinder to let them die. In any case, many of the poor of London feared the city's often brutal and filthy hospitals so much that they preferred to die in peace at home rather than seek help. As the disease spread, bodies piled up in makeshift morgues each evening.

By the time the epidemic burnt itself out in the winter of 1832, more than 55,000 people had died from it across Great Britain, more than 6,500 in London alone. Cholera would continue to break out periodically across the country over the next 20 years. Then, in 1853, the disease returned to Britain's capital with a vengeance, killing more than 10,000 people over the next two years.

In 1854, John Snow, a doctor in London, finally confirmed through his investigations that the epidemic was being spread by dirty drinking water. Although the exact nature of cholera would still not be understood for another three decades, the crucial link between disease and poor public sanitation, due in large part to rapid industrial development, had been firmly established. As industrialization brought rapid growth to Britain's manufacturing towns and cities, workers had poured into the new industrial centers, where they lived in filthy, over-crowded slum tenements and totally overwhelmed the medieval sewage and water facilities then in use.

THE URBAN MIDDLE CLASS

If you want to see a monument to the satisfaction and self-assurance of the middle-class civilization that was evolving in the industrial cities of northern England at this time, you could do no better than to look at Leeds Town Hall. Completed in 1858, this gigantic neoclassical and baroque edifice boasts a 225-foot-tall (69-m-tall) clock tower. At the building's center is a gorgeously decorated 125-foot-long (38-m-long) concert hall, awash with stained glass, marble, bronze, and gold. To the wealthiest citizens of the era, the construction of such a glamorous and expensive building in Leeds was a statement of civic pride and poise.

From 1700 to 1840, Leeds had grown from a small town of 10,000 people to a bustling metropolis of 150,000, with the city's textile mills, machine tool workshops, and leather and pottery factories at the center of the north's industrial expansion. Leeds merchants produced 30 percent of Britain's woolen goods. A network of railroad lines connected Leeds with Manchester, Liverpool, Sheffield, and the other towns that formed the belt of manufacturing prosperity running across midland Britain from west to east.

COKETOWN

Published in 1854, Charles Dickens's novel *Hard Times* provides one of the most famous accounts of Britain's mid-nineteenth-century industrial cities. "Coketown" is the ugly, polluted mill town in which much of the story is set, an unnatural purgatory where callous "self-made man" Josiah Bounderby cruelly treats the badly paid and overworked factory workers. In the following excerpt, Dickens accuses many of his well-to-do readers of being complicit in the exploitation of Coketown's poor:

> It was a town of red brick, or of brick that would have been red if the smoke and ashes had allowed it; but as matters stood, it was a town of unnatural red and black, like the painted face of a savage. It was a town of machinery and tall chimneys, out of which interminable serpents of smoke trailed themselves for ever and ever, and never got uncoiled. It had a black canal in it, and a river that ran purple with ill-smelling dye, and vast piles of building full of windows where there was a rattling and a trembling all day long, and where the piston of the steam-engine worked monotonously up and down, like the head of an elephant in a state of melancholy madness. It contained several large streets all very like one another,

What had arisen in towns like Leeds was a new industrial governing class, a class built on the dynamic entrepreneurship of the textile and steam revolutions and completely unconnected to the old aristocratic, landowning elite. At its pinnacle were the great mill and factory owners, the shipyard barons, and the railroad tycoons. A rung down the ladder was the next class, the engineers and architects and surveyors, the merchant

and many small streets still more like one another, inhabited by people equally like one another, who all went in and out at the same hours, with the same sound upon the same pavements, to do the same work, and to whom every day was the same as yesterday and to-morrow, and every year the counterpart of the last and the next.

These attributes of Coketown were in the main inseparable from the work by which it was sustained; against them were to be set off, comforts of life which found their way all over the world, and elegancies of life which made, we will not ask how much of the fine lady, who could scarcely bear to hear the place mentioned. The rest of its features were voluntary, and they were these.

You saw nothing in Coketown but what was severely workful. If the members of a religious persuasion built a chapel there—as the members of eighteen religious persuasions had done—they made it a pious warehouse of red brick. . . . All the public inscriptions in the town were painted alike, in severe characters of black and white. The jail might have been the infirmary, the infirmary might have been the jail, the town-hall might have been either, or both, or anything else, for anything that appeared to the contrary in the graces of their construction. . . .*

* Charles Dickens, *Hard Times* (1854). New York: Oxford University Press, 2008, pp. 26-27.

middlemen, and the legions of accountants and lawyers who handled the red tape generated by commerce. Below them were the small shopkeepers and grocers, the clerks, foremen, and artisans—in essence, the community of white-collar employees who ran the day-to-day affairs on the factory and workshop floor. There were great differences between these tiers in terms of wealth and status, and yet in an important sense, they thought of themselves as belonging to a single class—the middle class between the landed gentry and the poor—with its own shared values and aspirations.

The urban middle class made its home in the genteel outer suburbs of the new cities. You can still see the fine townhouses and villas built by affluent businessmen and tradesmen in places like Leeds today. Middle-class city dwellers were ferocious consumers, spending their money on new commercial goods—crockery, silverware, pottery, fine clothes, and furniture—which had once been luxury items exclusively for the wealthy but were now within the budget of even modest white-collar households. The most prosperous among them demonstrated their civic spirit with lavish charitable endowments, building churches, hospitals, parks, and places of entertainment for the masses. They were proud of their cities and proud of the wealth and stability their entrepreneurship had brought. In many respects, they had every right to be proud. But they also ignored a good deal of human misery and injustice right at their own doorsteps.

THE SQUALOR OF THE SLUMS

"The people of the abyss" is what the American writer Jack London would later call the slum dwellers of industrial cities. To travel into the poorest quarters of industrial centers like Manchester, Liverpool, and London after time spent in the airy, clean, and spacious middle-class suburbs was like venturing to a different planet. To house their industrial workers who had flooded into the new factory towns at the beginning of the 1800s, mill owners and other employers had thrown up whole

This nineteenth-century photograph of a slum in Victorian London clearly displays the overcrowding in such areas, where light, air, and decent living conditions were hard to come by.

quarters of cheap, densely packed terraces. Rainwater seeped through their thin damp walls, and mold gathering in the cellars became a serious health risk. Space was so inadequate that a family of 10 people might have to occupy a single room and a single bed. There was often no fresh water and rarely any toilet facilities other than a large, deep hole dug in the courtyard that might be shared by hundreds of other people. Needless to say, infestation was typical, and rats and other vermin lived well on the raw sewage. To give some sense of the health consequences of this slum existence, it is worth noting that, from 1820 to 1830, the life expectancy of a poor person living in a British city fell on average from 35 to 29 years old.

Part of the problem was the almost complete lack of any institutions of local government in the new industrial cities, which had risen so quickly from their tiny medieval origins that no representative bodies were in place to raise taxes, enforce regulations, or demand reforms. It was not until 1835 that the Municipal Corporations Act was passed, creating local councils, elected by middle-class voters, with the right to raise revenues. Councils like these raised money for health and sanitary reform, and prevented some of the worst abuses of corrupt landlords.

The councils, however, were often slow to act, even in the face of mass human despair and squalor. A prevailing feeling at the time among many wealthier people was that to assist the poor would only encourage them to have as many children as possible and that their hard-earned taxes should not subsidize the lifestyles of those unable to look after themselves. Some within the middle class believed that poverty was a moral failing and that the poor had chosen the lifestyle they found themselves in. They pointed to the enormous quantities of alcohol consumed in Britain's cities—200 million quarts (189 million liters) of beer per year in London alone—as evidence of the vice and misbehavior of the urban slum dwellers. While it is true that rampant alcoholism ruined many lives within the poverty-stricken quarters, it is not all that surprising that many people, viewing their daily existence in such wretched conditions, would find escape in a bottle.

The Demand for Reforms

It was a truly beautiful day. A clear, blue summer sky, not a cloud in sight, that was very different from the drizzly overcast weather most Lancastrians had come to take for granted. No wonder, then, that so many people made their way to St. Peter's Field, just outside Manchester, on August 16, 1819. The atmosphere was friendly, even carnival-like, but orderly. Contingents of hundreds and thousands arrived throughout the morning from the city's boroughs and the towns and villages surrounding the great cotton metropolis. The men dressed smartly in their best suits, the women and children in their Sunday finery. The organizers had been insistent: Everyone attending must be sober, tidy, and peaceful. This great display of political protest had to send the message to London that ordinary working-class people were responsible enough to

TO HENRY HUNT, ESQ.

The Peterloo Massacre occurred on St. Peter's Field in Manchester, England, on August 16, 1819. After British cavalry charged into a crowd who had peacefully gathered to demand parliamentary representation, 15 people were killed and approximately 400 to 700 were injured.

deserve emancipation. By noon, approximately 60,000 people had gathered on St. Peter's Field, about half the population of Greater Manchester.

There were several reasons for the protest. Lancashire was undergoing hard times. With the end of the Napoleonic Wars four years earlier, demand for textiles had slackened. But as factory wages fell and employees were let go, the British government had introduced a high tariff on imports of foreign grain in order to protect the profits of aristocratic landlords at home. The price of bread, the staple of most ordinary people's

diet, had shot up. No welfare system existed to support working families who, through no fault of their own, could not
afford to feed themselves. Worse, the people of Manchester
did not have a voice in the decisions that affected their lives.
Despite being the center of Britain's industrial renaissance, the
city sent no members of Parliament to London. The electoral
map of the nation, which had not been altered for hundreds of
years, no longer reflected the reality of the industrial age. The
protesters on St. Peter's Field intended to stage a mock parliamentary election, one that would have no legal consequence
but would illustrate in powerful symbolic terms the injustice
of their situation.

The authorities, however, did not see the mass assembly
outside Manchester in nearly the same spirit. To them, this
was not a peaceful call for reform; this was a rehearsal for an
uprising. These same authorities well remembered the French
Revolution (1789–1799), that bloody onslaught against the
ruling classes across the English Channel. The wealthy landowners of Lancashire were frightened by this demonstration
and sought to suppress it as quickly as possible. Manchester's
magistrates were ordered to arrest the ringleaders of the protest and disperse the crowd. Because no organized police force
existed in 1819 to assist the magistrates in their duties, they
turned to the army instead. Several hundred men of the local
county yeomanry, a unit of mounted volunteer soldiers—
hotheaded, contemptuous of what they called the "rabble,"
and in some cases drunk—were called to help.

A little after one o'clock, some of the yeoman cavalry
moved into the crowd to clear a path for the magistrates.
Frustrated by the sheer mass of people blocking their horses'
way, they drew their sabers and began to slash at the protesters
below. Alarmed and angry, some in the crowd started to jeer
and throw stones. The inexperienced soldiers lost their tempers
and charged, hacking their way through the sea of bodies with

(continues on page 96)

MICHAEL SADLER (1780–1835) AND JOHN BRIGHT (1811–1889)

The careers of Michael Sadler and John Bright illustrate how the battle for reform during the Industrial Revolution was extremely complicated. Supporters of one type of reform could reject others.

Sadler, a wealthy gentleman farmer from Derbyshire, believed passionately in the natural right of the pre-industrial aristocracy to continue to govern Britain, but along with that right also came a responsibility to look after the best interests of the poor and exploited. He opposed all changes to the composition of the House of Commons, such as were proposed in the 1832 Reform Bill. Yet Sadler also condemned the enclosure of common land and insisted that the state should introduce welfare assistance to the poverty-stricken Irish population. Most famously of all, he devoted much of his public life to the cause of child labor. It was thanks to his efforts that the first serious legislation regulating children's working con-ditions in factories was introduced in 1833. Sadler spoke eloquently in Parliament of the desperate condition of child laborers:

> The parents rouse them in the morning and receive them tired and exhausted after the day has closed; they see them droop and sicken, and, in many cases, become cripples and die, before they reach their prime; and they do all this, because they must otherwise starve. It is a mockery to contend that these parents have a choice. They choose the lesser evil, and reluctantly

resign their offspring to the captivity and pollution of
the mill.*

By contrast, the radical John Bright devoted much of
his life to the cause of parliamentary reform. The son of a
self-made Quaker textile manufacturer, Bright campaigned
for the abolition of protective tariffs on imported grain,
which kept food prices artificially high. He accepted as just
the demands for universal suffrage and the secret ballot.
Bright, however, objected to factory reform, believing that
the government had no right to insist on minimum working
conditions for employees. Bright saw the world from the
point of view of the industrialist; he rejected the old aristocratic order, but he believed that state interference in the
free market was counterproductive and would lead to falling
profits and the general decline in everyone's fortunes. The
parliamentary record *Hansard* reports Bright as saying during
a debate on one of the Factory Acts:

> No-one would accuse [me] of a want of sympathy with
> the working classes . . . but if [Parliament] now armed
> the workmen against the capitalists by fixing by law ten
> hours, or any other number of hours for the duration of
> labor, and thus interfered with the established custom of
> the Kingdom, [this would be] most injurious and destruc-
> tive to the best interests of the country . . . it was con-
> trary to all the principles of sound legislation; it was a
> delusion practiced upon the working classes.**

---

* Michael Sadler, "Speech in the House of Commons," March 16,
1832. http://hansard.millbanksystems.com/commons/1847/
feb/10/factories-bill#S3V0089P0_18470210_HOC_14.

** Quoted in Lee T. Wyatt, *The Industrial Revolution*. Westport,
Conn.: Greenwood Press, 2009, pp. 229-230.

(continued from page 93)
their swords. The crowd panicked. More soldiers wielding fixed bayonets blocked their line of retreat. The scene was chaos; even the officers lost control of the situation. One cavalry commander appealed to his men, in vain, to pull back: "For shame, gentlemen: what are you about? The people cannot get away!"[1] Within 10 minutes the shattered crowd had fled. Fifteen people had been stabbed, crushed, or trampled to death, with hundreds more injured. Riots broke out throughout Manchester for several days.

The British government tried 10 of the protest leaders for the crime of sedition, and five were sentenced to prison. None of the soldiers were punished for their offenses. Indeed, the Prince of Wales wrote a congratulatory letter to them for their defense of law and order. But the popular outcry after the massacre was deafening. The incident soon became known as "Peterloo," in a mocking reference to the Battle of Waterloo that had been fought a few years earlier. If the authorities had hoped that their actions that Sunday would silence demands for reform, they proved mistaken. Over the next 30 years, other agitators across the country, angry at the government's complacent attitude toward political and social injustices, rose in protest. Many of the evils they condemned—unhealthy factories, overcrowded cities—had been created by industrialization, and yet it was the advances in movement and communication produced by the Industrial Revolution that enabled them to organize on a national basis.

POLITICAL REFORM

Despite the government's defiance in the wake of the Peterloo Massacre, 1819 was in fact a watershed moment. Many moderate parliamentarians, shaken by the state's use of violence against the protesters, were worried that further refusals to consider reform would only intensify the pressure from below. Perhaps it would not be 60,000 people assembling in Manches-

This illustration from 1831 shows a demonstration of London's reformers, who demanded the right to vote and the reform of electoral districts after the House of Lords rejected the Reform Act. Parliament would pass the act in 1832, which introduced wide-ranging changes to the British electoral system.

ter next time, but 600,000 people, armed and angry, marching on London instead. Concessions seemed more sensible than resistance. Besides which, the injustice of the parliamentary system was becoming harder and harder to ignore. The existing arrangements for electing MPs were a mockery of the shape of industrial Britain. Not only were the factory towns of the north and Midlands woefully underrepresented, but in order to vote in most constituencies, a man had to own farmland worth at least £2, or 40 shillings. That left even prosperous middle-class town dwellers outside the franchise, let alone poor workers.

(After the reforms of 1832, men no longer had to own agricultural land, but could own urban real estate instead.)

One key obstacle to change, however, was the vehement opposition of King George IV. Moderates hoping to introduce reform had to wait until his death in 1830 and the ascension to the throne of his more progressive-minded brother William IV. After three blocked attempts and a promise by the new

LIFE FOR MANCHESTER'S WORKING POOR

Friedrich Engels (1820-1895) is most famous for *The Communist Manifesto*, his 1848 collaboration with the revolutionary writer Karl Marx, but he also made an important contribution to social reform with his exposé of the lives of the industrial urban poor, *The Condition of the Working Class in England* (1844). Although Engels was from a wealthy merchant family and would in time become a partner in a prosperous Manchester textile firm, he was appalled by the desperate lives led in the city's poorest quarters. In this excerpt he describes one of the most wretched areas of "Cottonopolis":

> Southward from Great Ancoats Street, lies a great, straggling, working-men's quarter, a hilly, barren stretch of land, occupied by detached, irregularly built rows of houses or squares, between these, empty building lots, uneven, clayey, without grass and scarcely passable in wet weather. The cottages are all filthy and old. . . . Along both sides of the stream, which is coal-black, stagnant and foul, stretches a broad belt of factories and working-men's dwellings, the latter all in the worst condition. . . .

king that if necessary he would use his powers to force the act through Parliament no matter what, a Reform Bill was finally made law in 1832. The bill completely reorganized the electoral map of the country, abolishing many tiny pre-industrial constituencies and granting representation for the first time to 43 towns and cities, including Manchester, Leeds, Sheffield, and Birmingham. It also granted the vote to urban residents

> The most horrible spot . . . lies on the Manchester side, immediately south-west of Oxford Road, and is known as Little Ireland. In a rather deep hole, in a curve of the Medlock and surrounded on all four sides by tall factories and high embankments, covered with buildings, stand two groups of about two hundred cottages, built chiefly back to back, in which live about four thousand human beings, most of them Irish. The cottages are old, dirty, and of the smallest sort, the streets uneven, fallen into ruts and in part without drains or pavement; masses of refuse, offal and sickening filth lie among standing pools in all directions; the atmosphere is poisoned by the effluvia from these, and laden and darkened by the smoke of a dozen tall factory chimneys. A horde of ragged women and children swarm about here, as filthy as the swine that thrive upon the garbage heaps and in the puddles. In short, the whole rookery furnishes such a hateful and repulsive spectacle as can hardly be equaled. . . . The race that lives in these ruinous cottages, behind broken windows, mended with oilskin, sprung doors, and rotten doorposts, or in dark, wet cellars, in measureless filth and stench, in this atmosphere penned in as if with a purpose, this race must really have reached the lowest stage of humanity.*
>
> ---
>
> * Friedrich Engels, *The Condition of the Working Class in England* (1844). New York: Oxford University Press, 2009, pp. 72-73.

who lived in properties worth at least £10. At a stroke this extended the franchise to about one in seven adult males. (British women would have to wait almost another century for their chance to vote.)

Still, the Reform Act of 1832 left many radicals deeply unsatisfied. The wealthy town-dwelling middle class had gotten what it wanted, but the factory worker too poor to qualify for voting rights was still denied a political voice. Agitation for more democratization of the system continued. It found its most important expression in the Chartist movement, named after the "Great Charter" of demands that almost two million people signed. Chartists wanted to grant the vote to all working men over 21, regardless of wealth, and to introduce the secret ballot. (At the time, all voting had to be done in public, which created opportunities for bribery and intimidation.) Chartism, the first mass-participatory labor movement in Britain, used the new technologies of industrialization, especially the cheap distribution of newspapers and pamphlets by the railroad, to rally support. The Chartist wave fizzled out in the late 1840s in disappointment, with Parliament still rejecting all its demands. During the next half-century, however, successive British governments adopted most of the points on the Great Charter. Popular democracy for the industrial working class was slow to come, but patience and persistence won out in the end.

SOCIAL AND LABOR REFORM

While middle-class industrialists were eager to see political reform (for their own benefit) in the 1820s, they had no sympathy for social and legal reforms that would regulate their businesses or raise additional taxes for state welfare. Despite the wretched conditions in factories and slums, they believed that government interference in the affairs of the market was inefficient and unjust and often quoted Adam Smith's doctrine of the "invisible hand" in their defense (though from his writings it seems clear that Smith himself would probably not have agreed with them).

What industrialists did want the government to do was to crack down hard on workers who were organizing (or "combining") to try to force their employers to improve wages and conditions under the threat of strike action. The 1799 Combination Act, further strengthened in 1825, made it illegal to form what today would be called labor unions and punished workers who deliberately "conspired" with one another with heavy prison sentences or transportation to a penal colony. The so-called Tolpuddle Martyrs, six Devonshire workmen who were sent to Australia for the crime of having sworn an oath to collectively organize, became symbolic of the lack of rights of ordinary British employees. It was not until 1867 that the government finally accepted that labor unions were legitimate organizations.

Early efforts to overhaul the country's welfare laws were designed more for the benefit of middle-class taxpayers than for the underprivileged themselves. In 1834, the New Poor Law was passed, creating a national system of workhouses to which men, women, and children were to be sent if they were too destitute to care for themselves. The act was popular among the prosperous voters enfranchised by the 1832 Reform Act, because it was cheap and regarded poverty as a moral vice for which punishment was the logical remedy. To the poor, however, the workhouse, which was more a prison than a place of shelter, became a symbol of terror and degradation. Charles Dickens would depict its dismal conditions in such works as his 1838 novel *Oliver Twist*. The workhouse cast a long shadow; the modern welfare state did not really emerge in Britain until the mid-twentieth century.

Yet some reforms did come more quickly. The appalling conditions in which child laborers were forced to work in factories became a national scandal in the 1820s. Thanks to the efforts of MPs like Michael Sadler, the 1833 Factory Act was passed, the first really significant attempt to regulate working conditions in British industry. This act banned the employment of children under nine years old and put a nine-hour cap on the working day of older boys and girls. Mill and factory owners were also required to provide schooling for all child employees. Additionally, the act provided, for the first time, funding for full-time government inspectors to visit and scrutinize workplaces. Although many abuses persisted, the days of rampant exploitation of workers in industrial Britain were coming to an end. Over the next 60 years, a series of subsequent acts and reforms tightened health and safety regulations even more for all employees, adults as well as children.

Similarly, reforms in public health in cities did finally take place. In the 1860s, for instance, the Manchester town council approved construction of a modern sewer system. The city also appointed a medical officer to inspect slum tenements. Across Britain, new housing regulations demanded that landlords provide all-new houses with windows for ventilation and backyard space. A clean water supply became generally available. Public hospitals were opened to prevent the spread of infectious diseases. Progress was uneven, but life in "Cottonopolis" and other poorer quarters in industrial cities was much more bearable in the later 1800s than it had been when Friedrich Engels wrote his famous account of the city's slums.

An Industrialized
World

Treason. That was the crime that Samuel Slater was committing when he stepped off the London quayside onto the boat for America on September 13, 1789—or at least, it was treason according to the British government. For many years, would-be industrialists in the United States had been desperately trying to get information about British textile mills, machinery, and industrial management to cross the Atlantic. Bonuses of $100, a very large sum of money at the time, had been offered to anyone prepared to come to America to teach entrepreneurs in New York and Massachusetts how to manufacture in the British way. But London was determined to protect its trade secrets. All export of industrial machinery, plans, and technical knowledge was banned. Skilled engineers were refused permission to emigrate. As far as the British government was concerned, the

Industrial Revolution was to be permanently sealed off from the rest of the world.

Samuel Slater would have none of it. A 21-year-old poor farmer's son from Derbyshire, Slater had started life with few obvious prospects. But his intelligence and ambition had impressed the manager of one of Richard Arkwright's textile mills so much that he took the youngster on as an apprentice. Over the next several years, he developed a detailed working knowledge of the mill, its machinery, and its organization. Slater was eager to set up in business by himself, but the idea of competing with a man like Arkwright did not appeal to him. The lure of American money, however, was tempting. Knowing that he did not dare take any paper documents with him, for fear of search and arrest, Slater memorized the design of the mill. He disguised himself as a farmer and booked passage on a ship to New York City. After two months at sea, he arrived in Manhattan. After making contact with New England business-man Moses Brown, Slater and Brown opened up a textile mill modeled on Arkwright's in Rhode Island. Over the next 45 years, Slater invested in 13 other mills and died a millionaire. In the intervening time, thanks to his pioneering work, New England had become a center of industrial textile manufactur-ing to rival Lancashire's.

The British government's attempt to prevent the spread of industrialization was understandable, but ultimately futile. Unique conditions had allowed the Industrial Revolution to start in Britain, but once it had taken root in that country, there was no reason it could not be replicated elsewhere. Machinery could be copied, ideas borrowed and improved upon. Eventually realizing the pointlessness of trying to pre-vent the inevitable, the British began to deliberately export their know-how and technology across the world. The result was that the Industrial Revolution began to transform life thousands of miles away from its starting point. Factories, workshops, and great cities sprouted up along the Rhine River

The Industrial Revolution has transformed the world in many positive and negative ways. Industrial plants that caused great health and environmental problems, such as the Monkton Coke Works plant in Tyne and Wear, England, operated for decades without major improvements. The Monkton Coke Works were constructed in 1936 to provide jobs during the Great Depression. The plant closed in 1990 and was demolished in 1992.

estuary in Germany, in Japan, and across the Great Plains of the United States.

INDUSTRIALIZATION SPREADS ABROAD

One of the first places where British industrial ideas migrated was Belgium. A mere hop across the English Channel, Belgium was close at hand and also possessed many of the conditions that had allowed industry to grow in Britain in the first place. It had a large urban population; its workers had a tradition of textile craftsmanship; it had lots of excess capital for investment;

and perhaps most importantly, it sat on the same European coal seam as England. By the 1850s, Belgium had almost 50 blast furnaces and was exporting 76,000 tons (68,946 metric tons) of iron annually to Germany, and an extensive railroad network crisscrossed the small country.

Industrial growth in France was more patchwork. The country's economy remained rooted in agriculture well into the 1800s, and its people mostly continued to live in the countryside for far longer than in Britain. Yet even here there were pockets of dynamic expansion; Normandy, for instance, became a major center of modern textile production. The most important shift in European industrialization came, however, in the 1870s, when modern mining and factory techniques reached the coal- and iron-rich western provinces of Germany. German industrialists quickly matched, and then outpaced, their British counterparts. In 1870, Germany made only 13 percent of the world's manufactured products, less than half of Britain's share of the global market. By the eve of the First World War in 1914, Germany had overtaken Britain. The pioneers had been usurped.

This triumph was bittersweet, however, for across the Atlantic the United States was outselling both Britain and Germany combined. By 1913, American industrialization had come a long way from the days of Samuel Slater. In the nineteenth century, America's vast size and resources had presented at first a considerable geographical obstacle; simply linking the country's people and products was a great challenge in its own right, made more complicated still by the political turmoil between North and South that eventually led to the American Civil War (1861–1865). Just four years after the end of that great conflict, however, the first transcontinental railroad line had been completed between the Atlantic and Pacific coasts, and the United States had more railroad track than the rest of the world put together.

America was at the heart of the so-called Second Industrial Revolution, which began in the 1850s. In that revolution, the original technologies of change—textile making, iron, and steam—began to make way for new processes and products; steel and light metal alloys, chemical and electrical engineering; and the internal combustion engine. By the beginning of the twentieth century, the United States was not just an economic rival (and superior) nation to Great Britain and other countries in Europe, it was the fulcrum of all further industrial expansion worldwide.

INDUSTRIALIZATION TODAY

Political revolutions—the American Revolution, the French Revolution—ultimately end. The Industrial Revolution never has. Although for convenience's sake, historians draw a line around 1850, as its first century of industrial development came to a close and its center of gravity gradually shifted away from the British Isles across the Atlantic, people alive at the time did not sense any slackening of the pace of change. On the contrary, things only seemed to be moving faster and getting more complicated. Already by the mid-1800s, industrial ideas had begun to migrate outside the West entirely, first in Japan and later in other parts of Asia, South America, and Africa. Russian peasant laborers poured into the new ironworks of St. Petersburg. Railroad lines linked India's teeming cities. Steamships carried coffee and sugar from Brazilian wharfs and refrigerated beef from Argentina's stockyards. Shantytowns of itinerant miners sprouted around the gold and diamond mines of South Africa.

Industrialization did not immediately and completely conquer the globe. As late as the 1950s, much of what we know today as the developing world, including China, South and Southeast Asia, sub-Saharan Africa, and South America, remained largely preindustrial. The great bulk of their populations were still living in small villages in the countryside and making a living from subsistence agriculture. But over the last half-century, even

(continues on page 110)

CHINA: NINETEENTH-CENTURY INDUSTRIALIZATION IN THE TWENTY-FIRST CENTURY

Just as Europe and North America went through rapid industrialization in the 1800s, so today countries like India and China are undergoing the same metamorphosis. Traditional rural societies in these Asian nations are turning into modern industrial economies, in much the same way as occurred in England 200 years ago. This transformation will bring new wealth and new opportunities to millions of poor people. But is it environmentally sustainable? As this 2007 article from *Mother Jones* argues, China's economic development is wreaking havoc with East Asia's fragile ecosystem:

> [Once,] the People's Liberation Army ritualistically fired shells at the Taiwan-controlled island of Quemoy; now, the mainland spews garbage that floats across the mile-and-a-quarter-wide channel and washes up on Quemoy's beaches at the rate of 800 metric tons [881 tons] a year. Acid rain caused by China's sulfur-dioxide emissions severely damages forests and watersheds in Korea and Japan and impairs air quality in the United States. Every major river system flowing out of China is threatened with one sort of cataclysm or another, including pollution, damming, diverting, and melting of the glacial source. . . .
>
> The growing Chinese taste for furs and exotic foods and pets is devastating neighboring countries' populations of gazelles, marmots, foxes, wolves, snow leopards, ibexes, turtles, snakes, egrets, and parrots, while its

appetite for shark fin soup is causing drastic declines in shark populations throughout the oceans; . . . the absence of the oceans' top predators is causing a resurgence of skates and rays, which are in turn destroying scallop fisheries along America's Eastern Seaboard. China's new predilection for sushi is even pricing Japan out of the market for bluefin tuna. Enthusiasm for traditional Chinese medicine, including its alleged aphrodisiacs, is causing huge declines in populations of hundreds of animals hunted for their organs. . . . China overtook the United States as the world's leading emitter of carbon dioxide in 2006.

Until 1998, China fed its wood mills trees from its own forests. That year, the middle reaches of the Yangtze River swelled with the region's biggest flood in more than 50 years, killing 3,000 people, destroying 5 million homes, and engulfing 52 million acres [21 million ha] of land. As winter approached months later, 14 million were still homeless. The land, it turned out, had no defense against erosion left. Lakes and wetlands that once would have absorbed some of the rain had been drained to create farmland, and the forests that once held topsoil in place had been harvested. Torrential rainwater carried the topsoil to the river and then down it, until its bed swelled with new sediment and the floodwater rose above its banks. As a result, China declared a logging ban on what little remained of its old-growth forests. Most environmentalists applauded the ban until they grasped its corollary: Chinese companies began harvesting other countries' trees on an even grander scale. . . .*

---

* Jacques Leslie, "The Last Empire: China's Pollution Problem Goes Global," *Mother Jones*, December 10, 2007. http://motherjones.com/environment/2007/12/last-empire-chinas-pollution-problem-goes-global.

(continued from page 107)
these remaining outposts of preindustrial society have begun to feel the effects of technological and organizational change.

In the years following World War II (1939–1945), nations such as Taiwan, South Korea, and Malaysia suddenly developed advanced industrial economies. Communities that had had sporadic contact with the outside world were connected physically (by the train, car, and airplane) and intangibly (by the radio, television, the telephone, and the Internet) in a global network of people and ideas. Multinational corporations took the consumer revolution to the Amazon jungle and the Sahara desert. Populations moved in unprecedented numbers, and usually toward one another. In 2008, it was estimated that more than half of the world's people were living in towns and cities for the first time in history. We are all part of the Industrial Revolution now.

Is that a good thing or not? Some of the obvious benefits of industrialization are hard to argue with: higher standards of living, better foods and medicines, higher levels of education, greater on-average prosperity worldwide. Industrialization, however, can also produce dislocation, cruelty, and exploitation; the sweatshops of Cambodia and Nicaragua churning out T-shirts and sneakers today bear an uncomfortable resemblance to the pre-Factory Act mills of Lancashire. Many economists, however, conclude that, in the long run, industrialization has bettered lives around the world. The reason that peasants have left the countryside in droves for generations to labor in sweatshops is because the work, however unpleasant, usually pays better than a life of backbreaking toil on the farm. Rural poverty might be more picturesque than urban squalor, but it does not create the same opportunities for long-term growth, both for the workers themselves and their children. As Nobel-winning economist Paul Krugman has suggested, "to oppose [industrialization] means that you are willing to deny desperately poor people the best chance they have of progress."[1]

A major problem facing the modern world is sustainability—maintaining the natural world and its limited resources. Industrial pollution, as seen here in this dump in Middlesbrough, North Yorkshire, England, is one of the major unfortunate by-products of the Industrial Revolution.

It is no accident that the great-grandchildren of European and American industrial workers, the men and women who once worked grueling factory shifts for low wages, now enjoy safe, clean, and generally affluent lives.

Whether the Earth can absorb the environmental consequences of global industrialization, however, is another story. From its beginnings, the Industrial Revolution placed an unprecedented strain on the planet's natural resources. As early as 1808, William Blake saw only "dark Satanic mills" where Lancashire's grimy smokestack factories were sprouting. In the 200 years since, the relentless demands of industrial production have ripped out of the Earth vast quantities of coal, oil, gas, ores, and precious metals—none of which are renewable. Carbon emissions from cars, planes, and factories into the atmosphere are widely believed to have raised the global mean temperature by more than one degree since 1900; if this trend continues, we are likely to see dramatic and possibly catastrophic climate change by the end of the twenty-first century.

Sustainability—the reorganization of our work and living practices to allow us to live within our ecological means without having to give up all of the material benefits that have been afforded by industrialization—will be the challenge of the years to come. The Arkwrights, Stephensons, Watts, and Adam Smiths of the coming generation will have to resolve a series of problems even more difficult than those that faced their predecessors, and with far more at stake.

CHRONOLOGY

1694	The Bank of England is founded, one of a number of financial innovations that helps to foster capitalist entrepreneurship in Britain.
1700	Population of Great Britain: 5 million; population of London: 600,000.
1701	Jethro Tull's mechanical seed drill allows farmers to plant crops more efficiently, paving the way for the British agricultural revolution.
1709	Abraham Darby pioneers the smelting of iron ore using coke rather than charcoal, dramatically lowering its cost.
1712	Thomas Newcomen builds the world's first commercially successful steam engine.
1733	John Kay invents the flying shuttle loom.
1761	The Bridgewater Canal opens.
1763	James Watt modifies a Newcomen steam engine, vastly improving its efficiency; the real "age of steam" now begins.
1764	Weaver James Hargreaves invents the spinning jenny.
1769	Textile manufacturer Richard Arkwright invents the water frame.
1776	Adam Smith publishes *The Wealth of Nations*.
1779	Samuel Crompton invents the spinning mule.
1785	Edmund Cartwright builds the steam-driven power loom, fully automating the process of weaving.
1803	The Napoleonic Wars begin (lasting till 1815).

1798   Thomas Malthus writes his *Essay on the Principle of Population*, warning of mass starvation if Britain's population continues to rise at its current rate.

1801   Population of Great Britain: 8 million; population of London: 1 million.

1804   Mining engineer Richard Trevithick builds the first working steam locomotive.

1811   Anti-machine Luddite riots break out in Nottingham.

1819   At the "Peterloo Massacre," soldiers charge a rally of unarmed political protesters outside Manchester, killing 15 people.

TIMELINE

1694
The Bank of England is founded, one of a number of financial innovations that helps to foster capitalist entrepreneurship in Britain.

1776
Adam Smith publishes *The Wealth of Nations.*

1694

1776

1700
Population of Great Britain: 5 million; population of London: 600,000.

1701
Jethro Tull's mechanical seed drill allows farmers to plant crops more efficiently, paving the way for the British agricultural revolution.

1763
James Watt modifies a Newcomen steam engine, vastly improving its efficiency; the real "age of steam" now begins.

1830   The world's first inter-city passenger-goods railroad begins operations from Liverpool to Manchester.

1832   The Reform Act gives the vote to middle-class British men; a cholera epidemic breaks out across Britain, killing more than 55,000 people.

1833   The first Factory Act, regulating working conditions for children, is passed.

1838   *The People's Charter*, demanding further political reforms, is published by the radical Chartist movement.

1844   Friedrich Engels publishes his book *The Condition of the Working Class in England*.

1785
Edmund Cartwright builds the steam-driven power loom, fully automating the process of weaving.

1801
Population of Great Britain: 8 million; population of London: 1 million.

1833
The first Factory Act, regulating working conditions for children, is passed.

1785

1851

1803
The Napoleonic Wars begin (lasting till 1815).

1830
The world's first inter-city passenger-goods railroad begins operations from Liverpool to Manchester.

1851
The Great Exhibition of the Works of Industry of All Nations opens in Hyde Park, London. Population of Great Britain: 20 million; population of London: 3 million.

1848   The Public Health Act creates local boards of
        health to try to improve sanitation and hygiene in
        Britain's industrial cities.

1851   The Great Exhibition of the Works of Industry
        of All Nations opens in Hyde Park, London.
        Population of Great Britain: 20 million;
        population of London: 3 million.

NOTES

CHAPTER 1

1. *Illustrated London News*, October 11, 1849.
2. Bernard Glassman, *Benjamin Disraeli: The Fabricated Jew in Myth and Memory*. Lanham, Md.: University Press of America, 2003, p. 2.
3. Edwin Fuller Torrey and Judy Miller, *The Invisible Plague: The Rise of Mental Illness from 1750 to the Present*. Piscataway, N.J.: Rutgers University Press, 2001, p. 104.

CHAPTER 3

1. "South Sea Bubble," Answers.com. http://www.answers.com/topic/the-south-sea-company.
2. Quoted in Lewis Saul Benjamin, *The South Sea Bubble*. London: D. O'Connor, 1921, p. 77.
3. "A Nation of Shopkeepers," The Phrase Finder. http://www.phrases.org.uk/meanings/12650.html.

CHAPTER 4

1. Quoted in Chris Andrews, *Britain, 1750–1900: Industry, Trade and Politics*. Cheltenham, U.K.: Nelson Thornes, 2002, p. 5.

CHAPTER 5

1. "Luddite Attack on Rawfolds Mill," April 1812. http://freepages.genealogy.rootsweb.ancestry.com/~maureenmitchell/luddites/luddites_william_cartwright_rawfolds_mill.htm.
2. "William Blake," Spartacus Educational. http://www.spartacus.schoolnet.co.uk/PRblake.htm.

CHAPTER 8

1. Quoted in "History of the Peterloo Massacre." http://www.peterloomassacre.org/history.html.

CHAPTER 9

1. Paul Krugman, "In Praise of Cheap Labor," Slate.com. March 21, 1997. http://www.slate.com/id/1918.

BIBLIOGRAPHY

Andrews, Chris. *Britain, 1750–1900: Industry, Trade and Politics.* Cheltenham, U.K.: Nelson Thornes, 2002.

Ashton, T.S. *The Industrial Revolution 1760–1830.* New York: Oxford University Press, 1997.

Bell-Irving, E.M. *Mayfield: The Story of an Old Wealden Village.* London: William Clowes, 1903.

Benjamin, Lewis Saul. *The South Sea Bubble.* London: D. O'Connor, 1921.

Dickens, Charles. *Hard Times* (1854). New York: Oxford University Press, 2008.

Engels, Friedrich. *The Condition of the Working Class in England.* New York: Oxford University Press, 2009.

"Eyewitness: The Great Exhibition, 1851." Timemachine.co.uk. Available online. URL: http://www.mytimemachine.co.uk/greatexhibition.htm.

Glassman, Bernard. *Benjamin Disraeli: The Fabricated Jew in Myth and Memory.* Lanham, Md.: University Press of America, 2003.

"The Great Exhibition of 1851." Available online. URL: http://myweb.tiscali.co.uk/speel/otherart/grtexhib.htm.

Higgins, Robert McR. "The 1832 Cholera Epidemic in East London." Available online. URL: http://www.mernick.org.uk//thhol/1832chol.html.

"History of the Peterloo Massacre." Available online. URL: http://www.peterloomassacre.org/history.html.

Horn, Jeff. *The Industrial Revolution: Milestones in Business History.* Westport, Conn.: Greenwood Press, 2007.

"The Industrial Revolution." Spartacus Educational. Available online. URL: http://www.spartacus.schoolnet.co.uk/Industrial Revolution.htm.

Krugman, Paul. "In Praise of Cheap Labor." Slate.com. March 21, 1997. Available online. URL: http://www.slate.com/id/1918.

Leslie, Jacques. "The Last Empire: China's Pollution Problem Goes Global." *Mother Jones*, December 10, 2007. Available online. URL: http://motherjones.com/environment/2007/12/last-empire-chinas-pollution-problem-goes-global.

Lines, Clifford. *Companion to the Industrial Revolution*. New York: Facts on File, 1990.

"Luddite Attack on Rawfolds Mill" (1812). Available online. URL: http://freepages.genealogy.rootsweb.ancestry.com/~maureenmitchell/luddites/luddites_william_cartwright_rawfolds_mill.htm.

Malthus, Thomas. *An Essay on the Principle of Population* (1798). New York: Oxford University Press, 2008.

"Minutes of the evidence taken before the Committee on the Factories" (1833). Available online. URL: http://www.historyhome.co.uk/peel/factmine/coulson.htm.

Morgan, Kenneth. *The Birth of Industrial Britain: Economic Change 1750–1850*. London: Longman, 1999.

Smith, Adam. *The Wealth of Nations*. New York: Oxford University Press, 2008.

Torrey, Edwin Fuller, and Judy Miller. *The Invisible Plague: The Rise of Mental Illness from 1750 to the Present*. Piscataway, N.J.: Rutgers University Press, 2001.

Wyatt, Lee T. *The Industrial Revolution*. Westport, Conn.: Greenwood Press, 2009.

FURTHER RESOURCES

BOOKS

Appleby, Joyce. *The Relentless Revolution: A History of Capitalism*. New York: W.W. Norton, 2010.

Daunton, Martin. *Progress and Poverty: An Economic and Social History of Britain 1700–1850*. New York: Oxford University Press, 1995.

Sale, Kirkpatrick. *Rebels Against the Future: The Luddites and Their War on the Industrial Revolution*. Reading, Mass.: Addison-Wesley, 1995.

Weightman, Gavin. *The Industrial Revolutionaries: The Making of the Modern World 1776–1914*. New York: Grove Press, 2009.

Wolmar, Christian. *Blood, Iron, and Gold: How the Railroads Transformed the World*. New York: PublicAffairs, 2010.

WEB SITES

Ironbridge: Birthplace of Industry
http://www.ironbridge.org.uk/

Museum of Science and Industry, Manchester, England
http://www.mosi.org.uk/

National Railway Museum, York, England
http://www.nrm.org.uk/

PICTURE CREDITS

PAGE

8: Getty Images
14: © Infobase Learning
20: The Bridgeman Art Library
27: Alamy
33: The Granger Collection
39: The Bridgeman Art Library
49: The Granger Collection
52: The Granger Collection
57: The Granger Collection
59: Science Museum, London, UK/The Bridgeman Art Library

69: National Railway Museum, York, North Yorkshire, UK/ The Bridgeman Art Library
77: Hulton Archives/Getty Images
84: The Granger Collection
89: The Bridgeman Art Library
92: Manchester Art Gallery, UK/ The Bridgeman Art Library
97: The Picture Desk
105: Alamy
111: Alamy

INDEX

ABOUT THE AUTHOR

ALAN ALLPORT grew up in Whiston, England, and moved to the United States in 1994. He received a doctorate in history from the University of Pennsylvania in 2007 and currently teaches at Princeton University. He lives near Philadelphia with his wife and their children, Thomas and Katharine. He is also the author of *Demobbed: Coming Home After the Second World War*, published by Yale University Press in 2009.